Temporal QoS Manageme
Cloud Workflow Systems

Temporal QoS Management in Scientific Cloud Workflow Systems

by

Xiao Liu, Yun Yang
Centre for Computing and Engineering Software Systems
Swinburne University of Technology, Australia

Jinjun Chen
Centre for Innovation in IT Services and Applications
University of Technology, Australia

AMSTERDAM • BOSTON • HEIDELBERG • LONDON • NEW YORK • OXFORD • PARIS
SAN DIEGO • SAN FRANCISCO • SINGAPORE • SYDNEY • TOKYO

ELSEVIER

Acquiring Editor: Todd Green
Development Editor: Robyn Day
Project Manager: Andre Cuello

Elsevier
225 Wyman Street, Waltham, MA 02451, USA

Library of Congress Cataloging-in-Publication Data
Application submitted

British Library Cataloguing-in-Publication Data
A catalogue record for this book is available from the British Library

ISBN: 978-0-12-397010-7

For information on all Elsevier publications
visit our website at elsevierdirect.com

This book has been manufactured using Print On Demand technology. Each copy is produced to order and is limited to black ink. The online version of this book will show color figures where appropriate.

Contents

Acknowledgements

The authors are grateful for discussions with Dr. Willem van Straten and Ms. Lina Levin from the Swinburne Centre for Astrophysics and Supercomputing for the pulsar searching scientific workflow. This work is partially supported by the Australian Research Council under Linkage Project LP0990393 and Discovery Project DP110101340.

Preface

Cloud computing is the latest market-oriented computing paradigm which can provide virtually unlimited scalable high-performance computing resources. As a type of high-level middleware services for cloud computing, cloud workflow systems are a research frontier for both cloud computing and workflow technologies. Cloud workflows often underlie many large-scale data/computation-intensive e-science applications such as earthquake modelling, weather forecast and astrophysics. At the build-time modelling stage, these sophisticated processes are modelled or redesigned as cloud workflow specifications which normally contain the functional requirements for a large number of workflow activities and their non-functional requirements such as Quality of Service (QoS) constraints. At the run-time execution stage, cloud workflow instances are executed by employing the supercomputing and data sharing ability of the underlying cloud computing infrastructures. In this book, we focus on scientific cloud workflow systems.

In the real world, many scientific applications need to be time constrained, i.e. they must be completed by satisfying a set of temporal constraints such as local temporal constraints (milestones) and global temporal constraints (deadlines). Meanwhile, task execution time (or activity duration), as one of the basic measurements for system performance, often needs to be monitored and controlled by specific system management mechanisms. Therefore, how to ensure satisfactory temporal correctness (high temporal QoS), i.e. how to guarantee on-time completion of most, if not all, workflow applications, is a critical issue for enhancing the overall performance and usability of scientific cloud workflow systems.

At present, workflow temporal verification is a key research area which focuses on time-constrained large-scale complex workflow applications in distributed high-performance computing environments. However, existing studies mainly emphasise monitoring and detection of temporal violations (i.e. violations of temporal constraints) at workflow run-time; there is still no comprehensive framework that can support the whole life cycle of time-constrained workflow applications in order to achieve high temporal QoS. Meanwhile, cloud computing adopts a market-oriented resource model, i.e. cloud resources such as computing, storage and network are charged by their usage. Hence, the cost for supporting temporal QoS (including both time overheads and monetary cost) should be managed effectively in scientific cloud workflow systems.

This book presents a novel probabilistic temporal framework and its strategies for cost-effective delivery of high QoS in scientific cloud workflow systems (or temporal framework for short in this book). By investigating the limitations of conventional temporal QoS-related research, our temporal framework can provide a systematic and cost-effective support for time-constrained scientific cloud workflow applications over their whole life cycles. With a probability-based temporal consistency model, there are three major components in the temporal framework: Component 1 – temporal constraint setting; Component 2 – temporal consistency monitoring; Component 3 – temporal violation handling. Based on investigation and analysis, we present some new concepts and develop a set of innovative strategies and algorithms towards cost-effective delivery of high temporal QoS in scientific cloud workflow systems. Case studies, comparisons, quantitative evaluations and/or mathematical proofs are presented for the evaluation of each component. These demonstrate that our new concepts, innovative strategies and algorithms for the temporal framework can significantly reduce the cost for the detection and handling of temporal violations while achieving high temporal QoS in scientific cloud workflow systems.

Specifically, at scientific cloud workflow build time, in Component 1, a statistical time-series pattern-based forecasting strategy is first conducted to predict accurate duration intervals of scientific cloud workflow activities. Afterwards, based on the weighted joint normal distribution of workflow activity durations, a probabilistic setting strategy is applied to assign coarse-grained temporal constraints through a negotiation process between service users and service providers, and then fine-grained temporal constraints can be propagated along scientific cloud workflows in an automatic fashion. At scientific cloud workflow run-time, in Component 2, the state of scientific cloud workflow execution towards specific temporal constraints, i.e. temporal consistency, is monitored constantly with the following two steps: first, a minimum probability time redundancy-based temporal checkpoint selection strategy determines the workflow activities where potential temporal violations take place; second, according to the probability-based temporal consistency model, temporal verification is conducted on the selected checkpoints to check the current temporal consistency states and the type of temporal violations. In Component 3, detected temporal violations are handled with the following two steps: first, an adaptive temporal violation handling point selection strategy decides whether a temporal checkpoint should be selected as a temporal violation handling point to trigger temporal violation handling strategies; second, at temporal violation handling points, different temporal violation handling strategies are executed accordingly to tackle different types of temporal violations. In our temporal framework, we focus on metaheuristics-based workflow rescheduling strategies for handling statistically recoverable temporal violations.

The major contributions of this book are that we have presented a novel comprehensive temporal framework which consists of a set of new concepts, innovative strategies and algorithms for supporting time-constrained scientific applications over their whole life cycles in cloud workflow systems. With these, we can significantly reduce the cost of detection and handling of temporal violations whilst delivering high temporal QoS in scientific cloud workflow systems. This would eventually improve the overall performance and usability of cloud workflow systems because a temporal framework can be viewed as a software service for cloud workflow systems. Consequently, by deploying the new concepts, innovative strategies and algorithms, scientific cloud workflow systems would be able to better support large-scale sophisticated e-science applications in the context of cloud economy.

Xiao Liu, Jinjun Chen and Yun Yang

About the Authors

Xiao Liu received his PhD degree in Computer Science and Software Engineering from the Faculty of Information and Communication Technologies at Swinburne University of Technology, Melbourne, Australia, in 2011. He received his Master's and Bachelor's degrees from the School of Management, Hefei University of Technology, Hefei, China, in 2007 and 2004, respectively, all in Information Management and Information Systems. He is currently a postdoctoral research fellow in the Centre for Computing and Engineering Software System at Swinburne University of Technology. His research interests include workflow management systems, scientific workflows, cloud computing, business process management and quality of service.

Jinjun Chen received his PhD degree in Computer Science and Software Engineering from Swinburne University of Technology, Melbourne, Australia, in 2007. He is currently an Associate Professor in the Faculty of Engineering and Information Technology, University of Technology, Sydney, Australia. His research interests include scientific workflow management and applications, workflow management and applications in Web service or SOC environments, workflow management and applications in grid (service)/cloud computing environments, software verification and validation in workflow systems, QoS and resource scheduling in distributed computing systems such as cloud computing, service-oriented computing, semantics and knowledge management, and cloud computing.

Yun Yang received a Master of Engineering degree from the University of Science and Technology of China, Hefei, China, in 1987, and a PhD degree from The University of Queensland, Brisbane, Australia, in 1992, all in computer science. He is currently a full Professor in the Faculty of Information and Communication Technologies at Swinburne University of Technology, Melbourne, Australia. Prior to joining Swinburne as an Associate Professor in late 1999, he was a Lecturer and

Senior Lecturer at Deakin University from 1996 to 1999. Before that, he was a Research Scientist at DSTC — Cooperative Research Centre for Distributed Systems Technology — from 1993 to 1996. He also worked at Beihang University in China during 1987–88. He has published about 200 papers in journals and refereed conferences. His research interests include software engineering; p2p, grid and cloud computing; workflow systems; service-oriented computing; Internet computing applications; and CSCW.

1 Introduction

This book presents a novel probabilistic temporal framework to address the limitations of conventional temporal research and the new challenges for lifecycle support of time-constrained e-science applications in cloud workflow systems. The novel research reported in this book is concerned with the investigation of how to deliver high temporal Quality of Service (QoS) from the perspective of cost-effectiveness, especially at workflow run-time. A set of new concepts, innovative strategies and algorithms are designed and developed to support temporal QoS over the whole lifecycles of scientific cloud workflow applications. Case study, comparisons, quantitative evaluations and/or theoretical proofs are conducted for each component of the temporal framework. This would demonstrate that with our new concepts, innovative strategies and algorithms, we can significantly improve the overall temporal QoS in scientific cloud workflow systems.

This chapter introduces the background, motivations and key issues of this research. It is organised as follows. Section 1.1 gives a brief introduction to temporal QoS in cloud workflow systems. Section 1.2 presents a motivating example from a scientific application area. Section 1.3 outlines the key issues of this research. Finally, Section 1.4 presents an overview of the remainder of this book.

1.1 Temporal QoS in Scientific Cloud Workflow Systems

Cloud computing is a latest market-oriented computing paradigm [12,41]. Gartner estimated the revenue of the Worldwide cloud services is $58.6 billion in 2009, and it is forecast to reach $68.3 billion in 2010, and projected to reach $148.8 billion in 2014[1]. International governments such as the United States, the United Kingdom, Canada, Australian and New Zealand governments take cloud services as an opportunity to improve business outcomes through eliminating redundancy, increasing agility and providing ICT services at a potentially cheaper cost [1,29,33]. Cloud refers to a variety of services available on the Internet that deliver computing functionality on the service provider's infrastructure. A cloud is a pool of virtualised computer resources and may actually be hosted on such as grid or utility computing environments [8,68]. It has many potential advantages which include the ability to scale to meet changing user demands quickly;

---

[1] http://www.gartner.com/it/page.jsp?id=1389313

Temporal QoS Management in Scientific Cloud Workflow Systems. DOI: 10.1016/B978-0-12-397010-7.00001-X separation of infrastructure maintenance duties from users; location of infrastructure in areas with lower costs for real estate and electricity; sharing of peak-load capacity among a large pool of users and so on. Given the recent popularity of cloud computing, and more importantly the appealing applicability of cloud computing to the scenario of data and computation intensive scientific workflow applications, there is an increasing demand to investigate scientific cloud workflow systems. For example, scientific cloud workflow systems can support many complex e-science applications such as climate modelling, earthquake modelling, weather forecasting, disaster recovery simulation, astrophysics and high energy physics [32,93,97]. These scientific processes can be modelled or redesigned as scientific cloud workflow specifications (consisting of such things as workflow task definitions, process structures and QoS constraints) at the build-time modelling stage [32,62]. The specifications may contain a large number of computation and data-intensive activities and their non-functional requirements such as QoS constraints on time and cost [103]. Then, at the run-time execution stage, with the support of cloud workflow execution functionalities, such as workflow scheduling [105], load balancing [13] and temporal verification [20], cloud workflow instances are executed by employing the supercomputing and data-sharing ability of the underlying cloud computing infrastructures with satisfactory QoS.

One of the research issues for cloud workflow systems is how to deliver high QoS [20,26,40]. QoS is of great significance to stakeholders, namely service users and providers. On one hand, low QoS may result in dissatisfaction and even investment loss of service users; on the other hand, low QoS may risk the service providers of out-of-business since it decreases the loyalty of service users. QoS requirements are usually specified as quantitative or qualitative QoS constraints in cloud workflow specifications. Generally speaking, the major workflow QoS constraints include five dimensions, namely time, cost, fidelity, reliability and security [103]. Among them, time, as one of the most general QoS constraints and basic measurements for system performance, attracts many researchers and practitioners [61,110]. For example, a daily weather forecast scientific cloud workflow, which deals with the collection and processing of large volumes of meteorological data, has to be finished before the broadcasting of a weather forecast programme every day at, for instance, 6:00 p.m. Clearly, if the execution time of workflow applications exceeds their temporal constraints, the consequence will usually be unacceptable to all stakeholders. To ensure on-time completion of these workflow applications, sophisticated strategies need to be designed to support high temporal QoS in scientific cloud workflow systems.

At present, the main tools for workflow temporal QoS support are temporal checkpoint selection and temporal verification which deal with the monitoring of workflow execution against specific temporal constraints and the detection of temporal violations [21]. However, to deliver high temporal QoS in scientific cloud workflow systems, a comprehensive temporal framework which can support the whole lifecycles, viz. from build-time modelling stage to run-time execution stage, of time-constrained scientific cloud workflow applications needs to be fully investigated.

1.2 Motivating Example and Problem Analysis

In this section, we present an example in Astrophysics to analyse the problem for temporal QoS support in scientific cloud workflow systems.

1.2.1 Motivating Example

The Parkes Radio Telescope (http://www.parkes.atnf.csiro.au/), one of the most famous radio telescopes in the world, serves institutions around the world. The Swinburne Astrophysics group (http://astronomy.swinburne.edu.au/) has been conducting pulsar searching surveys (http://astronomy.swin.edu.au/pulsar/) based on the observation data from the Parkes Radio Telescope. The Parkes Multibeam Pulsar Survey is one of the most successful pulsar surveys to date. The pulsar searching process is a typical scientific workflow which involves a large number of data- and computation-intensive activities. For a single searching process, the average data volume (not including the raw stream data from the telescope) is over 4 terabytes and the average execution time is about 23 hours on Swinburne's high-performance supercomputing facility (http://astronomy.swinburne.edu.au/supercomputing/).

For the convenience of discussion, as depicted in Figure 1.1, we illustrate only the high-level workflow structure and focus on one path out of the total of 13 parallel paths for different beams (the other parallel paths are of similar nature and denoted by cloud symbols). The average durations (normally with large variances) for high-level activities (those with sub-processes underneath) and three temporal constraints are also presented for illustration. Given the running schedules of Swinburne's supercomputers and the observing schedules for the Parkes Radio Telescope (http://www.parkes.atnf.csiro.au/observing/schedules/), an entire pulsar searching process, i.e. a workflow instance, should normally be completed in 1 day, i.e. an overall temporal constraint of 24 hours, denoted as $U(SW)$ in Figure 1.1.

Generally speaking, there are three main steps in the pulsar searching workflow. The first step is data collection (about 1 hour), data extraction and transfer (about 1.5 hours). Data from the Parkes Radio Telescope streams at a rate of 1 gigabit per second and different beam files are extracted and transferred via gigabit optical fibre. The second step is data pre-processing. The beam files contain the pulsar signals which are dispersed by the interstellar medium. *De-dispersion* is used to counteract this effect. A large number of de-dispersion files are generated according to different choices of trial dispersions. In this scenario, 1,200 is the minimum number of dispersion trials and normally takes 13 hours to complete. For more dispersion trials, such as 2,400 and 3,600, either longer execution time is required or more computing resources need to be allocated. Furthermore, for binary pulsar searching, every de-dispersion file needs to undergo an *Accelerate* process. Each de-dispersion file generates several accelerated de-dispersion files and the whole process takes around 1.5 hours. For instance, if we assume that the path with 1,200 de-dispersion

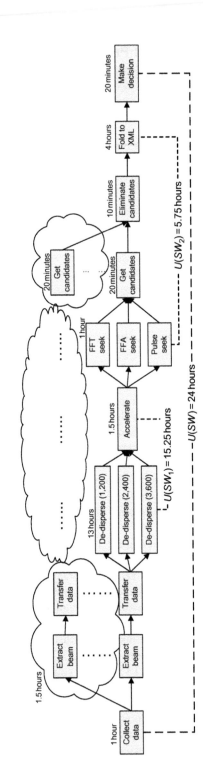

Figure 1.1 Example of scientific workflow for pulsar searching in astrophysics.

files is chosen, then a temporal constraint of 15.25 hours, denoted as $U(SW_1)$, usually should be assigned for the data pre-processing step. The third step is pulsar seeking. Given the generated de-dispersion files, different seeking algorithms can be applied to search for pulsar candidates, such as *FFT Seek*, *FFA Seek* and single *Pulse Seek*. For the instance of 1,200 de-dispersion files, it takes around 1 hour for FFT seeking to seek all the candidates. Furthermore, by comparing the candidates generated from different beam files in the same time session (around 20 minutes), some interference may be detected and some candidates may be eliminated (around 10 minutes). With the final pulsar candidates, the original beam files are retrieved to find their feature signals and fold them to XML files. The *Fold to XML* activity usually takes around 4 hours. Here, a temporal constraint of 5.75 hours, denoted as $U(SW_2)$, usually should be assigned. Finally, the XML files will be inspected manually (by human experts) or automatically (by software) to facilitate the decision making on whether a possible pulsar has been found or not (around 20 minutes).

1.2.2   Problem Analysis

Based on the above example, we can see that to guarantee on-time completion of the entire workflow process, the following problems need to be addressed.

1. Setting temporal constraints. Given the running schedules, a global temporal constraint, i.e. the deadline $U(SW)$ of 24 hours, needs to be assigned. Based on that, with the estimated durations of workflow activities, two other coarse-grained temporal constraints $U(SW_1)$ and $U(SW_2)$ are assigned as 15.25 and 5.75 hours, respectively. These coarse-grained temporal constraints for local workflow segments can be defined based on the experiences of service providers (e.g. the estimated activity durations) or the requirements of service users (e.g. QoS requirements). However, fine-grained temporal constraints for individual workflow activities, especially those with long durations such as *De-dispersion* and seeking algorithms, are also required in order to support fine-grained control of workflow executions. Meanwhile, the relationship between the high-level coarse-grained temporal constraints and their low-level fine-grained temporal constraints should be investigated so as to keep the consistency between them.

   Therefore, a temporal constraint setting component should be able to facilitate the setting of both coarse-grained and fine-grained temporal constraints in scientific cloud workflow systems. Meanwhile, as the prerequisite, an effective forecasting strategy for scientific cloud workflow activity durations is also required to ensure the accuracy of the setting results[2].

2. Monitoring temporal consistency state. Due to the complexity and uncertainty of the dynamic scientific cloud workflow system environments, the violations of fine-grained temporal constraints (the overrun of expected individual activity durations) may occur. Therefore, temporal consistency states need to be kept under constant monitoring to detect and handle potential violations in a timely fashion. For example, during the second step of data pre-processing, delays may occur in a *De-dispersion* activity that needs to

---

[2] Actually, since estimated activity duration is one of the most important data for the temporal framework, an effective forecasting strategy is required not only for setting temporal constraints but also for its subsequent components such as checkpoint selection, temporal verification and violation handling.

process terabytes of data or consumes more than 13 hours computation time. Here, for example, we assume that the *De-dispersion* activity takes 14.5 hours (a delay of 90 minutes, i.e. around 10% over the mean duration), then given $U(SW_1)$ of 15.25 hours, there would only be 45 minutes left for the *Accelerate* activity which normally needs 1.5 hours. Another example is that during the third step of pulsar seeking, we assume that the overall duration for the *FFT Seek*, *Get Candidates* and *Eliminate Candidates* activities is 108 minutes (a delay of 18 minutes, i.e. around 20% over the mean duration). In such a case, given $U(SW_2)$ of 5.75 hours, there will probably be a 3-minute delay if the subsequent activity completes on time. In both examples, time delays occurred and potential temporal violations may take place.

Therefore, based on the above two examples, we can see that monitoring of temporal consistency is very important for the detection of temporal violations. Effective and efficient strategies are required to monitor temporal consistency of scientific cloud workflow execution and detect potential violations as early as possible before they become real major overruns.

3. Handling temporal violations. If temporal violations like the two examples mentioned above are detected, temporal violation handling strategies are normally required. However, it can be seen that the temporal violations in the two examples are very different. In the first example with $U(SW_1)$, even if we expect the *Accelerate* activity can be finished in 10 minutes less than its mean duration (around 10% less than the mean duration, i.e. finished in 80 minutes), there would still be a 35-minute time deficit. Therefore, in such a situation, at that stage some temporal violation handling strategies should be executed to decrease the duration of the *Accelerate* activity to at most 45 minutes – for instance, by rescheduling the Task-to-Resource assignment or recruiting additional resources in order to maintain temporal correctness. Cleary, in such a case, a potential temporal violation is detected in which temporal violation handling is necessary. As in the second example with $U(SW_2)$, the 3-minute time deficit is a small fraction compared with the mean duration of 4 hours for the *Fold to XML* activity. Actually, there is a probability that it can be automatically compensated for since it only requires the *Fold to XML* activity to be finished 1.25% shorter than its mean duration. Therefore, in such a situation, though a temporal violation is detected, temporal violation handling may be unnecessary. Hence, an effective decision-making strategy is required to determine whether a temporal violation handling is necessary or not when a temporal violation is detected.

If a temporal violation handling is determined as necessary, temporal violation handling strategies will be executed. In scientific cloud workflow systems, every computing resource may be charged according to its usage. Therefore, besides the effectiveness (the capability of compensating occurred time deficits), the cost of the temporal violation handling process should be kept as low as possible. Therefore, on one hand, different levels of temporal violations should be defined. For example, for the above-mentioned two temporal violations, the first one with larger time deficit (i.e. 35 minutes) will normally require heavy-weight temporal violation handling strategies such as recruitment of additional resources, whilst the second one with smaller time deficit (i.e. 3 minutes) could be handled by light-weight strategies or even by self-recovery (i.e. without any treatment). On the other hand, the capability and cost of different temporal violation handling strategies should be investigated so that when specific temporal violations have been detected, the handling strategies with the required capability but with lower cost can be applied accordingly.

Therefore, for the purpose of cost-effectiveness, a decision-making process on temporal violation handling is required when a temporal violation is detected. Meanwhile, a set of cost-effective temporal violation handling strategies must be designed and developed so as to meet the requirements of different levels of fine-grained temporal violations.

1.3 Key Issues of This Research

This book investigates the deficiencies of existing research work on the lifecycle support of temporal QoS in scientific cloud workflow systems. First, there lacks a comprehensive temporal framework to support the whole lifecycle of time-constrained cloud workflow applications; secondly, the management cost for high temporal QoS should be proactively controlled by the design of cost-effective strategies for each component of the framework. With a probability-based temporal consistency model, there are three major components in our temporal framework: Component I − setting temporal constraints; Component II − monitoring temporal consistency; Component III − handling temporal violations.

Specifically, at scientific cloud workflow build time, in Component I, temporal constraints including both global temporal constraints for entire workflow processes (deadlines) and local temporal constraints for workflow segments and/or individual activities (milestones) are required to be set as temporal QoS constraints in cloud workflow specifications. The problem for the conventional QoS constraint setting strategies lies in three aspects: first, estimated workflow activity durations (based on user experiences or simple statistics) are often inaccurate in cloud workflow system environments; second, these constrains are not well balanced between user requirements and system performance; third, the time overheads of the setting process are non-trivial, especially for large numbers of local temporal constraints. To address the above issues, a statistical time-series pattern-based forecasting strategy is first investigated to predict the duration intervals of cloud workflow activities. Afterwards, based on the weighted joint normal distribution of workflow activity durations, a probabilistic setting strategy is applied to assign coarse-grained temporal constraints through a negotiation process between service users and service providers, and then the fine-grained temporal constraints can be propagated along scientific cloud workflows in an automatic fashion, i.e. with very small time overheads.

At scientific cloud workflow run-time, in Component II, the state of cloud workflow execution towards specific temporal constraints, i.e. temporal consistency, is monitored constantly by the checkpoint selection and temporal verification component. The two major limitations of conventional checkpoint selection and temporal verification are as follows: first, the selection of multiple types of checkpoints and the verification of multiple types of temporal consistency states incur huge cost although most of them are actually unnecessary; second, though the violations of multiple temporal consistency states can be verified, there is no clear indication for the level of temporal violations, i.e. it does not support the quantitative measurement of temporal violations. To address the above issues, with our probability-based temporal consistency model, the probability range for statistically recoverable and non-recoverable temporal violations is defined in the first place. Afterwards, we monitor cloud workflow executions through the following two steps: first, a minimum probability time redundancy-based temporal checkpoint selection strategy determines the activity points where potential temporal violations take place; second, probability temporal consistency-based temporal verification is conducted on a checkpoint to check the current temporal consistency state and the types of temporal violations, i.e. recoverable or non-recoverable.

Finally, in Component III, detected temporal violations are handled. The conventional temporal verification philosophy holds that temporal violation handling should be triggered on every checkpoint, i.e. whenever a temporal violation is detected. However, the number of checkpoints for large-scale scientific workflow applications is often huge in dynamic cloud computing environments, and thus results in significant cost in the handling of temporal violations. Therefore, we design a cost-effective adaptive temporal violation handling point selection strategy to further determine whether a checkpoint should be selected as a temporal violation handling point, i.e. whether temporal violation handling is necessary. Afterwards, when temporal violation handling points are selected, some temporal violation handling strategies are triggered to tackle the detected temporal violations.

So far, temporal violation handling strategies in scientific cloud workflow systems have not been well investigated, and the existing strategies are either of low performance or high cost. Therefore, in our temporal framework, an innovative temporal violation handling strategy is defined which consists of three levels of temporal violations (from minor to major) and their corresponding violation handling strategies (from weak capability to strong capability). In such a case, different levels of temporal violations can be handled according to the capability of different temporal violation handling strategies with appropriate costs. Among many other factors, we focus on cost-effective light-weight metaheuristics-based workflow rescheduling strategies for statistically recoverable temporal violations. Specifically, with the design of a general two-stage local workflow rescheduling strategy, two representative metaheuristic algorithms, including Genetic Algorithm (GA) and Ant Colony Optimisation (ACO), are adapted and implemented as candidate temporal violation handling strategies.

1.4 Overview of This Book

In particular, this book deals with the design of a comprehensive temporal framework which includes a set of new concepts, strategies and algorithms for the support of high QoS over the whole.

In Chapter 2, we introduce the related work on temporal QoS in workflow systems and analyse their limitations. Specifically, a temporal consistency model is used to define temporal consistency states; a temporal constraint setting is to assign both global and local temporal constraints at workflow build time; temporal checkpoint selection and temporal verification are the two main steps for monitoring of workflow execution and detection of temporal violations; temporal violation handling compensates the existing time deficits by temporal violation handling strategies.

In Chapter 3, we present a prototype scientific cloud workflow system SwinDeW-C (Swinburne Decentralised Workflow System for Cloud) which serves as the simulation environment for all the experiments demonstrated later in this book.

In Chapter 4, the high-level description of our probabilistic temporal framework is presented. The foundation of the temporal framework is a novel probability-based temporal consistency model where fine-grained temporal consistency states can be quantitatively measured by probability confidence values. In order to facilitate the lifecycle support of high temporal QoS for scientific cloud workflow applications, our temporal framework is composed of three main components. The main technical details of the framework are presented separately in three components: Component I for temporal constraint setting, Component II for temporal consistency monitoring and Component III for temporal violation handling.

Component I consists of two chapters, namely Chapters 5 and 6.

In Chapter 5, a statistical time-series pattern-based forecasting strategy for scientific cloud workflow activity duration intervals is described. By investigating the typical requirements in cloud computing environments, a novel time-series segmentation algorithm named *K-MaxSDev* is presented to discover statistical time-series patterns and their associated turning points. After that, accurate duration intervals can be predicted. Comparison experiments with representative forecasting strategies are demonstrated to evaluate the effectiveness of our strategy.

In Chapter 6, a probabilistic temporal constraint setting strategy is presented. Based on the joint weighted normal distribution model, the execution time of a workflow instance or workflow segments can be estimated effectively and efficiently with the support of four basic building blocks: sequence building block, iteration building block, parallelism building block and choice building block. After that, the coarse-grained temporal constraints are first assigned through a negotiation process between service users and service providers based on either a time-oriented or probability-oriented manner. When the coarse-grained temporal constraints are set, the fine-grained temporal constraints for each individual workflow activities can be derived and propagated in an automatic fashion. Therefore, the time overheads and computation cost for temporal constraints setting are much smaller compared with conventional manual settings. The effectiveness of the strategy is demonstrated through a case study.

Component II consists of Chapter 7.

In Chapter 7, the existing state-of-the-art checkpoint selection and temporal verification strategy are modified to adapt to our probability-based temporal consistency model so that now only one type of checkpoint needs to be selected instead of multiple types, and only one type of temporal consistency state needs to be verified instead of multiple types. Accordingly, the minimum probability time redundancy-based checkpoint selection strategy and probability temporal consistency-based temporal verification strategy are provided. The mathematical proof has demonstrated that our adapted strategy is of the same necessity and sufficiency as the existing state-of-the-art checkpoint selection strategy but with better cost-effectiveness.

Component III consists of Chapters 8 and 9.

In Chapter 8, an adaptive temporal violation handling point selection strategy is presented. Temporal violation handling point selection is a novel idea from our latest study on workflow temporal verification. Based on the necessary and sufficient checkpoints, temporal violation handling point selection further selects a subset of these checkpoints where the probability of temporal violations is higher than the specific threshold, i.e. temporal violation handling is indeed necessary. Motivated by adaptive testing techniques and requirements of cost-effectiveness, our temporal violation handling point selection strategy can select many fewer violation handling points than conventional strategies while maintaining satisfactory temporal QoS. In such a case, the overall cost for handling temporal violations can be significantly reduced.

In Chapter 9, an overview of temporal violation handling strategies is presented. Given the basic requirements of *automation* and *cost-effectiveness*, we design a general light-weight two-stage local workflow rescheduling strategy which features a two-stage searching process with metaheuristic algorithms. Such a general rescheduling strategy can ensure the balance between the execution of workflow instances with temporal violations and those without temporal violations. With such a general rescheduling strategy, two metaheuristic algorithms, GA and ACO, are adapted and implemented, and then their performances are compared in four different measurements including the optimisation rate of makespan, the optimisation rate of cost, the time-deficit compensation rate and the CPU time. Afterwards, the three-level temporal violation handling strategy designed in our temporal framework is presented and followed by comprehensive evaluation on its performance and cost. As detailed in Section 9.4, the handling strategy consists of three levels of temporal violations (level I, level II and level III) and their corresponding handling strategies, *PTDA* (probability time-deficit allocation), *ACOWR* (ACO based two-stage workflow local rescheduling) and *PTDA + ACOWR* (the hybrid of *PTDA* and *ACOWR*).

Finally, in Chapter 10, we first make an overall cost analysis for each component in our temporal framework. Then, we summarise the new ideas discussed in this book, the major contributions of this research and consequent further research works.

2 Literature Review and Problem Analysis

This chapter reviews the existing work related to temporal QoS organised as follows. Section 2.1 gives a general introduction of workflow temporal QoS. Section 2.2 reviews the temporal consistency model. Section 2.3 reviews the temporal constraint setting. Section 2.4 reviews the temporal checkpoint selection and temporal verification. Section 2.5 reviews the temporal violation handling. In each section, the problems with the current work are analysed along the line.

2.1 Workflow Temporal QoS

In a cloud environment, there are a large number of similar or equivalent resources provided by different service providers. Cloud service users can select suitable resources and deploy them for cloud workflow applications. These resources may provide the same functionality but optimise different QoS measures [86]. Meanwhile, different service users or applications may have different expectations and requirements. Therefore, it is insufficient for a scientific cloud workflow system to consider only functional characteristics of workflow applications. QoS requirements such as time limits (temporal constraints) and budget limits (cost constraints) for cloud workflow execution also need to be managed by scientific cloud workflow systems. Service users must be able to specify their QoS requirements of scientific cloud workflows at build time. Then, the actions taken by the cloud workflow systems at run-time must be chosen according to the original QoS requirements.

Generally speaking, there are five basic dimensions for cloud workflow QoS, namely time, cost, fidelity, reliability and security [51,103]. Time is a basic measurement of system performance [2,3,54]. For workflow systems, the makespan often refers to the total time overheads required for completing the execution of a workflow. The total cost often refers to the monetary cost associated with the execution of workflows including such factors as the cost of managing workflow systems and the usage charge of cloud resources for processing workflow activities. Fidelity refers to the measurement related to the quality of the output of workflow execution. Reliability is related to the number of failures of workflows. Security refers to confidentiality of the execution of workflow tasks and the trustworthiness of resources. Among them, time, as a basic measurement of performance and

Temporal QoS Management in Scientific Cloud Workflow Systems. DOI: 10.1016/B978-0-12-397010-7.00002-1

general non-functional requirement, has attracted most of the attention from researchers and practitioners in such areas as Software Engineering [89], Parallel and Distributed Computing [48,76] and Service-Orientated Architectures [38]. In this book, we focus on time, i.e. we investigate the support of high temporal QoS in scientific cloud workflow systems.

In the real world, most scientific processes are assigned specific deadlines in order to achieve their scientific targets on time. For those processes with deterministic process structures and fully controlled underlying resources, individual activity durations, i.e. the completion time of each activity, are predictable and stable. Therefore, process deadlines can normally be satisfied through a build-time static scheduling process with resource reservation in advance [39,105]. However, stochastic processes such as scientific workflows are characterised with dynamic changing process structures due to the nature of scientific investigation. Furthermore, with a vast number of data and computation intensive activities, complex workflow applications are usually deployed on dynamic high-performance computing infrastructures, e.g. cluster, peer-to-peer, grid and cloud computing [5,70,97,100]. Therefore, ensuring cloud workflow applications are finished within specific deadlines is a challenging issue. In fact, this is why temporal QoS is emphasised more in large-scale distributed workflow applications compared with traditional centralised workflow applications [2].

In the following sections, we will introduce the current work related to temporal QoS in cloud and conventional workflow systems.

2.2   Temporal Consistency Model

Temporal consistency denotes the consistency between build-time temporal QoS specifications and run-time workflow execution states, namely temporal correctness. A temporal consistency model defines different temporal consistency states where a temporal consistency state measures the execution state of a workflow instance against specific temporal constraints. It is the fundamental standard for temporal verification [18]. Intuitively, according to true or false temporal correctness, the states of temporal consistency can be defined as either temporal consistency states or temporal inconsistency states. However, this coarse-grained definition is apparently too weak for conducting fine-grained analysis and control. Therefore, in recent years, a multiple-discrete-states-based temporal consistency model has been widely adopted. In order to avoid huge temporal violation handling costs, besides conventional temporal consistency state denoted as Strong Consistency (SC), multiple discrete states differentiate three fine-grained states in the conventional temporal inconsistency state: Weak Consistency (WC), Weak Inconsistency (WI) and Strong Inconsistency (SI) [18]. However, since multiple discrete states are defined based on the basic static time attributes such as the maximum, minimum and mean durations of individual workflow activities, complex statistical analysis models cannot be well supported. Meanwhile, such a model still suffers the following limitations: first, with qualitative expressions, it is difficult for service users to understand the level of current temporal violations without sufficient background knowledge and system information; second, with the definitions of four coarse-grained temporal consistency states, some unnecessary temporal verification costs may be incurred. For example, if the current temporal consistency state is SI, and the temporal verification starts from SC, then WC and then WI, it will cost three times more to identify the current temporal consistency state.

Given the definition for different temporal consistency states, different levels of temporal violations, such as the WC violations (the violations of WC), can be defined accordingly. However, another critical issue with current temporal consistency models is that they do not consider the capabilities of specific temporal violation handling strategies employed in a scientific cloud workflow system. In such a case, it is unclear which temporal violation handling strategy should be applied when a certain level of temporal violation is detected, and thus the result will probably be the failure of temporal violation handling (e.g. when a light-weight temporal violation handling strategy is applied for a major temporal violation) or the unnecessary loss of time and budget (e.g. when a heavy-weight temporal violation handling strategy is applied for a minor temporal violation). Therefore, for the purpose of cost-effectiveness, the definition of temporal violations should be able to facilitate the selection of light-weight temporal violation handling strategies (for minor temporal violations) and heavy-weight temporal violation handling strategies (for major temporal violations).

2.3 Temporal Constraint Setting

Temporal constraint setting assigns temporal constraints in scientific cloud workflow specifications at build time [17]. Recent studies support the assumption that temporal constraints are pre-defined and focus only on run-time monitoring of temporal consistency states. However, the fact is that efforts made at run-time will be mostly in vain without build-time setting of high-quality temporal constraints. The reason is obvious since the purpose of temporal verification is to identify potential violations of temporal constraints to minimise the temporal violation handling cost. Therefore, if temporal constraints are of low quality themselves, temporal violations may often take place no matter how much effort has been dedicated to run-time temporal verification. In the real world, service users normally have limited knowledge of the performance of the underlying cloud services except their general descriptions. In such a case, it is difficult for users to estimate the activity durations or workflow makespan. Therefore, the temporal constraints assigned by service users are mainly based on their own interests with ignorance of the real system performance such as system load [61]. Meanwhile, service users usually prefer to assign only one or several coarse-grained temporal constraints. However, for the purpose of effectively monitoring a large scale scientific cloud workflow, a large number of fine-grained temporal constraints are required along cloud workflow execution. Therefore, scientific cloud workflow systems need to derive fine-grained temporal constraints given the input of coarse-grained temporal constraints by service users [17,62].

For cloud workflow systems, the quality of temporal constraints can be measured by at least two basic criteria: (1) well balanced between user requirements and system performance; (2) well supported for both overall coarse-grained control and local fine-grained control. Generally speaking, there are two basic ways to assign QoS constraints: task-level assignment and workflow-level assignment [103]. Since the whole workflow process is composed of individual tasks, an overall workflow-level constraint can be obtained by the composition of task-level constraints. Conversely, task-level constraints can also be assigned by the decomposition of workflow-level constraints. However, different QoS constraints have their own characteristics and require in-depth research to handle different scenarios. Currently, the problem of temporal constraint setting in scientific cloud workflow systems has not been well investigated.

2.4 Temporal Consistency Monitoring

After temporal constraints are assigned at build time, a cloud workflow instance must be constantly monitored for temporal violations along the entire workflow execution at run-time. At present, temporal checkpoint selection and temporal verification are the two basic steps for run-time monitoring of temporal consistency states [16]. Temporal checkpoint selection is to select specific activity points along cloud workflow execution to conduct temporal verification on the fly [19]. Temporal verification checks the current temporal consistency state of cloud workflow execution according to the pre-defined temporal consistency model [18].

In recent years, many checkpoint selection strategies, from intuitive rule-based to sophisticated model-based, have been proposed [37,69,110]. The work in Ref. [37] takes every workflow activity as a checkpoint. The work in Ref. [69] selects the start activity as a checkpoint and adds a new checkpoint after each decision activity is executed. It also mentions a type of static activity point which is defined by users at the build-time stage. Since temporal verification inevitably produces extra cost, a Checkpoint Selection Strategy (CSS) aims to dynamically select only necessary and sufficient activity points to conduct temporal verification. Here, necessity means that only those activity points where real temporal inconsistency states take place are selected and sufficiency means that there are no omitted activity points [22]. Conventional CSS (e.g. setting checkpoints at the start time and end time of each activity or selecting each decision activity as a checkpoint) usually either chooses unnecessary checkpoints or misses some of them, or both [23]. To address such issues, a minimum time redundancy-based CSS is proposed in Ref. [22] which selects an activity point as a checkpoint only when a temporal violation is detected. Therefore, it is proved to be of both necessity and sufficiency. As for temporal verification, its effectiveness and efficiency are highly related to its corresponding temporal consistency model and CSS [16]. Taking the verification of WI as an example, with the multiple-states–based temporal consistency model and WI minimum time redundancy, only those activity points where WI violations take place are selected as checkpoints to further verify the temporal consistency states [18]. Furthermore, for multiple-states–based temporal consistency, the relationships between different temporal consistency states such as WC and WI, or WI and SI, can be reasoned to further improve the efficiency of temporal verification. The basic idea is that for a specific temporal constraint, if it is verified to be a higher consistency state, e.g. SC, then we do not need to check for WC, WI or SI, and so forth. This rule saves unnecessary costs for temporal verification [21].

At present, given a specific temporal consistency model, checkpoint selection and temporal verification are usually investigated together to suit the needs of different scenarios and improve the overall effectiveness and efficiency in monitoring run-time temporal consistency. However, due to the dynamic nature of cloud computing environments, violations of local temporal constraints (local violations for short) may often take place and result in a large number of checkpoints. Hence, according to current temporal verification strategy, the accumulated cost of temporal verification at all the selected checkpoints can eventually be huge. Therefore, a more cost-effective solution is required to reduce the whole cost while maintaining the performance of current state-of-the-art checkpoint selection and temporal verification strategies.

2.5 Temporal Violation Handling

After temporal verification, the current temporal consistency state is verified and, if a temporal violation is identified, the follow-up step is to handle such a violation, i.e. temporal violation handling. So far, the study on temporal violation handling is still in its infancy.

Temporal violation handling is very different from conventional violation handling which mainly deals with functional failures in workflow systems [46,88]. Usually, after functional failures are detected, a violation handling process such as rollback and recovery is triggered [10]. Another way to prevent functional failures is to run duplicate instances of the same workflows and hence, if one instance fails, the others can still be running. However, duplicate instances will result in huge management costs which can be several times higher than the necessary execution cost in general [30]. As for temporal violations, as a type of non-functional QoS failure, they cannot be handled after they actually take place since no actions in the real world can reduce the execution time of workflow activities after they are already finished. In fact, in a cloud computing environment, if a workflow application has exceeded its deadline (i.e. the global temporal constraint), the service provider can likely do nothing but pay the penalty according to its service contracts or negotiate with the service user for endurance, i.e. extra waiting time. Therefore, rather than relying on passive recovery, temporal violations need to be proactively prevented by temporal verification and temporal violation handling before actual large overruns take place [67]. In other words, effective handling of local temporal violations along workflow execution, rather than recovery of global temporal violations, must be investigated for the delivery of high temporal QoS in scientific cloud workflow systems.

The work in Ref. [87] introduces five types of workflow exceptions where temporal violation can be classified into deadline expiry. Meanwhile, three alternate courses of recovery action — no action (*NIL*), rollback (*RBK*) and compensate (*COM*) — are also presented. *NIL*, which counts on the automatic recovery of the system itself, is normally not acceptable for the 'risk-free' purpose. An *RBK*, unlike handling conventional system function failures, normally causes extra delays and makes current inconsistency states even worse. However, *COM*, i.e. time-deficit compensation, is believed to be a suitable recovery action for temporal violation.

One of the representative solutions introduced in Ref. [18] is a time-deficit allocation strategy (*TDA*) which compensates current time deficits by utilising the expected time redundancies of subsequent activities. However, since time deficit has not been truly reduced, this strategy can only delay the violations of some local constraints with no effectiveness on overall constraints, e.g. the deadlines. On the contrary, workflow rescheduling [106] can indeed make up a time deficit by expediting the execution of those not-yet-commenced workflow activities. However, since general workflow scheduling is an NP complete problem, extra cost is hence inevitable [105]. Up to now, there are few efforts dedicated to this topic. However, in order to deliver high temporal QoS in scientific cloud workflow systems, temporal violation handling plays a significant role. Therefore, it is important that cost-effective temporal violation handling strategies should be investigated. As for the measurement, the key criterion is their performance, i.e. how much time deficit can be compensated. Meanwhile, the cost of the compensation process (e.g. time overheads and monetary cost) should also be considered since it is unacceptable if the cost of the compensation process itself is significant, e.g. exceeding the expected cost of the penalty brought by those temporal violations.

3 A Scientific Cloud Workflow System

This chapter demonstrates a scientific cloud workflow system called SwinDeW-C [58,68,101]. The work presented in this book is being gradually implemented as system components and tested in SwinDeW-C, which is a cloud workflow system prototype built on SwinCloud, a cloud computing test bed. All the simulation experiments demonstrated in this book are conducted in our SwinCloud environment. The SwinCloud infrastructure and SwinDeW-C architecture are depicted in Figures 3.1 and 3.2, respectively.

SwinCloud is a cloud computing simulation test bed, on which SwinDeW-C is currently running. It is built on the computing facilities at the Swinburne University of Technology and takes advantage of the existing SwinGrid systems [100]. For example, the Swinburne Astrophysics Supercomputer Node (http://astronomy.swin.edu.au/supercomputing/) comprises 145 nodes of Dell Power Edge 1950 nodes, each with 2 quad-core Clovertown processors at 2.33 GHz (each processor is 64-bit low-volt Intel Xeon 5138), 16 GB RAM and 2×500 GB drives. We install VMware [96] on SwinGrid so that it can offer unified computing and storage resources. By utilising the unified resources, we set up data centres that can host applications. In the data centres, Hadoop [45] is installed to facilitate the MapReduce [42] computing paradigm and distributed data management.

In general, the types of cloud service can be classified as IaaS (Infrastructure as a Service), PaaS (Platform as a Service) and SaaS (Software as a Service). Meanwhile, from the system architecture perspective, the cloud architecture includes four basic layers from top to bottom: application layer (user applications), platform layer (middleware cloud services to facilitate the development/deployment of user applications), unified resource layer (abstracted/encapsulated resources by virtualisation) and fabric layer (physical hardware resources) [12]. Accordingly, the architecture of SwinDeW-C can also be mapped to the four basic layers. Here, we present the lifecycle of an abstract workflow application to illustrate the system architecture. Note that we focus on the system architecture; the introduction of the cloud management services (e.g. brokering, pricing, accounting and virtual machine management) and other functional components are omitted here but can be found in Ref. [68].

Users can easily gain access to the SwinDeW-C Web portal via any electronic device such as a PC, laptop, PDA or mobile phone as long as they are connected to the Internet. At the workflow build-time stage, given the cloud workflow modelling tool provided by the Web portal on the application layer, workflow applications are modelled by users as cloud workflow specifications (consisting of, for example,

Temporal QoS Management in Scientific Cloud Workflow Systems. DOI: 10.1016/B978-0-12-397010-7.00003-3

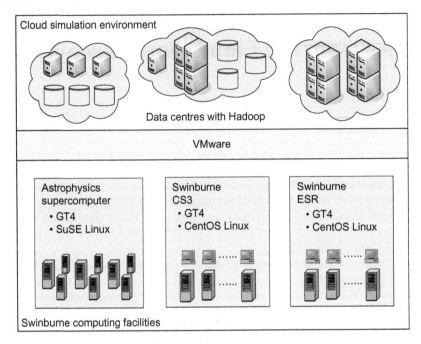

Figure 3.1 SwinCloud infrastructure.

task definitions, process structures and QoS constraints). After workflow specifications are created (static verification tools such as structure errors and QoS constraints may also be provided), they can be submitted to any one of the coordinator
peers in the platform layer. Here, an ordinary SwinDeW-C peer is a cloud service
node which has been equipped with specific software services similar to a
SwinDeW-G peer [100]. However, while a SwinDeW-G peer is deployed on
a stand-alone physical machine with fixed computing units and memory space, a
SwinDeW-C peer is deployed on a virtual machine of which the computing power
can scale dynamically according to the task request. As for the SwinDeW-C coordinator peers, they are super nodes equipped with additional workflow management
services and knowledge across different clouds than those of ordinary SwinDeW-C
peers.

At the run-time instantiation stage, the cloud workflow specification can be submitted to any of the SwinDeW-C coordinator peers. Afterwards, the workflow tasks
will be assigned to suitable peers through peer-to-peer (p2p)-based communication
between SwinDeW-C peers. Since the peer management (i.e. peer join, peer leave
and peer search, as well as the p2p-based workflow execution mechanism) is the
same as in the SwinDeW-G system environment, the detailed introduction is omitted here; it can be found in Ref. [100]. Before workflow execution, a coordinator
peer conducts an assessment on the submitted cloud workflow instance to determine whether it can be accepted or not, given the specified non-functional QoS
requirements under the current pricing model. It is generally assumed that

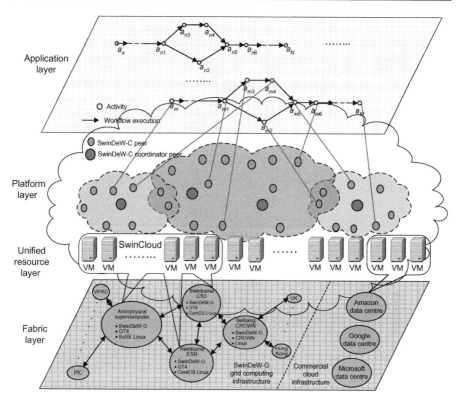

Figure 3.2 SwinDeW-C cloud workflow system architecture.

functional requirements can always be satisfied given the theoretically unlimited scalability of cloud. In cases where users need to run their own special programs, they can upload them through the Web portal and these programs can be automatically deployed in the data centre by the resource manager. Here, a negotiation process between the user and the cloud workflow service provider may be conducted if the submitted workflow instance is not acceptable to the workflow system due to an unacceptable offer on budget or deadline. The final negotiation result will be either compromised QoS requirements or a failed submission of the cloud workflow instance. If all the task instances have been successfully allocated (i.e. acceptance messages are sent back to the coordinator peer from all the allocated peers), a cloud workflow instance may be completed with satisfaction of both functional and non-functional QoS requirements (if they are without exceptions). Hence, a cloud workflow instance is successfully instantiated.

Finally, at the run-time execution stage, each task is executed by a SwinDeW-C peer. In cloud computing, the underlying heterogeneous resources are virtualised as unified resources (virtual machines). Each peer utilises the computing power provided by its virtual machine which can easily scale according to the request of workflow tasks. As can be seen in the unified resource layer of Figure 3.3,

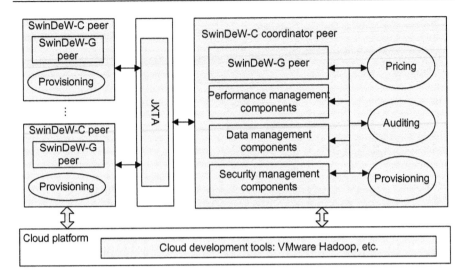

Figure 3.3 Architecture of SwinDeW-C peers.

SwinCloud is built on the previous SwinGrid infrastructure at the fabric layer. Meanwhile, some of the virtual machines can be created with external commercial IaaS cloud service providers such as Amazon, Google and Microsoft. During cloud workflow execution, workflow management tasks such as QoS management, data management and security management are executed by the SwinDeW-C peers. Users can gain the access to the final results as well as the execution information of their submitted workflow instances at any time through the SwinDeW-C Web portal.

As described above, SwinDeW-C is developed based on SwinDeW-G, where a SwinDeW-C peer has inherited most of the SwinDeW-G peer's components, including the components of task management, flow management, repositories and group management. Hence, a SwinDeW-G peer acts as the core of a SwinDeW-C peer, which provides the basic workflow management components and communication components between peers. However, some improvements are also made for SwinDeW-C peers to accommodate the cloud computing environment. The architecture of the SwinDeW-C peers is depicted in Figure 3.3.

First, in contrast to a SwinDeW-G peer, a SwinDeW-C peer runs on the cloud platform. The cloud platform is composed of unified resources, which refers to the computation and storage capabilities that a SwinDeW-C peer can dynamically scale up or down based on the applications' requirements. Unified resources are offered by cloud service providers and managed in resource pools, hence every SwinDeW-C peer has a provisioning component to dynamically apply and release the cloud resources. Meanwhile, through the SwinDeW-C coordinate peer, it can also scale out or in if necessary, i.e. to request the distribution of workflow activities to more or fewer SwinDeW-C peers in the same group. This is mainly realised through the Application Programming Interface (APIs) of VMware management tools.

Second, the resource pricing and auditing components are integrated into SwinDeW-C coordinator peers. Since different cloud service providers may offer different prices during the instantiation stage, a coordinator peer needs to have the pricing component to negotiate the prices with external service providers and set its own offered prices to its users. Meanwhile, since the cloud workflow system needs to pay for the usage of external cloud resources, an auditing component is required at the execution stage to record and audit the usage of cloud resources. These functionalities are mainly realised through the APIs of resource brokers and the external service provider's monitoring services such as Amazon CloudWatch (http://aws.amazon.com/cloudwatch/).

Last but not least, the coordinator peer of SwinDeW-C also has new functional components related to cloud workflow management. Specifically, for the requirements of different workflow QoS dimensions, components of performance management, data management and security management are added to the SwinDeW-C coordinator peer. Here, the performance management component mainly focuses on the workflow response time, i.e. the temporal management discussed in this book and also addresses the system throughput with some simple strategies. The data management component consists of the strategies working on two QoS dimensions, namely cost (on the data storage) and reliability (on the data replication). The security management component mainly focuses on trust management among the cloud services and the privacy protection of user information during the workflow execution. More details about these components can be found in Ref. [68] and are hence omitted here.

Based on the design discussed above, we have been building a primitive prototype of SwinDeW-C. The prototype is developed in Java and currently running on the SwinCloud simulation environment. In the SwinDeW-C prototype, we have inherited most of the SwinDeW-G functions and further implemented the new components of SwinDeW-C so that it can adapt to the cloud computing environment. Furthermore, we have built a Web portal for SwinDeW-C by which system users and administrators can access the cloud resources and manage the applications of SwinDeW-C. The Web portal provides many interfaces to support both system users and administrators for the following tasks.

Specifically, system users can:

- browse the existing data sets that reside in different cloud service providers' data centres;
- upload their application data to and download the result data from the cloud storage;
- create and deploy workflows to SwinDeW-C using the modelling tools;
- monitor workflow execution.

For system administrators:

- coordinate workflow execution by triggering scheduling strategies;
- manage application data by triggering data placement strategies; and
- handle functional and non-functional violations by triggering workflow exception handling strategies.

Some interfaces of the Web portal are shown in Figure 3.4.

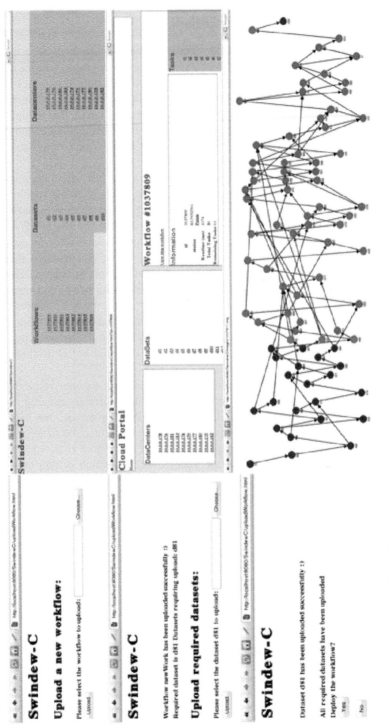

Figure 3.4 SwinDeW-C web portal.

4 Novel Probabilistic Temporal Framework

This book presents a novel comprehensive probabilistic temporal framework to address the limitations of conventional temporal verification and the new challenges for cost-effective lifecycle support of time-constrained scientific workflow applications in cloud workflow systems. This chapter presents a high-level description of our framework and its three major components with technical details described in the subsequent chapters.

This chapter is organised as follows. Section 4.1 presents the framework overview. Section 4.2 introduces the design of the first component, i.e. temporal constraint setting. Section 4.3 introduces the design of the second component, i.e. temporal consistency monitoring. Section 4.4 introduces the design of the third component, i.e. temporal violation handling.

4.1 Framework Overview

The aim of our novel temporal framework is to provide a cost-effective solution to deliver high temporal QoS in scientific cloud workflow systems. The temporal framework is designed to support the whole lifecycle of workflow instances, i.e. from the build-time modelling stage to the workflow run-time execution stage to successful completion. Specifically, in our temporal framework, the foundation is the probability-based temporal consistency model, and its capability is realised by three components that support workflow instances throughout their lifecycles, including temporal constraints setting, temporal consistency monitoring and temporal violation handling.

As depicted in Figure 4.1, our probabilistic framework consists of three components which can provide lifecycle support for high temporal QoS in scientific cloud workflow systems. The three inner cycles stand for the three important factors involved in the scientific cloud workflows: real-world applications, scientific workflows and cloud services. All the basic requirements for scientific cloud workflows come from real-world applications. Service users must first abstract real-world applications with the support of workflow modelling tools and then create the workflow specifications. With the workflow specifications (usually in the form of visualised workflow templates) submitted by the service users, scientific workflows are executed by the cloud workflow systems with the underlying cloud computing infrastructures. Cloud workflow systems, as a type of platform service themselves, can utilise many other cloud services that provide software services or computing

Temporal QoS Management in Scientific Cloud Workflow Systems. DOI: 10.1016/B978-0-12-397010-7.00004-5

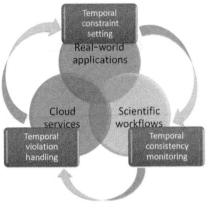

Figure 4.1 The probabilistic framework for temporal QoS.

services. Evidently, the execution of scientific cloud workflows is complex since scientific workflow instances usually have large-scale sophisticated processes that contain a large number of data- and computation-intensive activities. Meanwhile, the performance of scientific cloud workflow systems is uncertain since cloud services generally have highly dynamic performance in the cloud computing environments. Therefore, due to such process complexity and performance uncertainty, high temporal QoS cannot be easily achieved without a comprehensively designed framework to support the lifecycle of scientific cloud workflows. This is the fundamental motivation for our research work presented in this book.

The three components are organised in a cycle denoting that they are working in a way that supports the whole lifecycle of scientific cloud workflows.

The first component is temporal constraint setting, which assigns both global temporal constraints (temporal constraints for entire workflow instances) and local temporal constraints (temporal constraints for local workflow segments and individual workflow activities) in scientific cloud workflow specifications at workflow build time. At this stage, temporal constraints, as a type of QoS requirement, are to be specified in cloud workflow definitions. With other QoS constraints such as cost and security, these temporal constraints serve as critical criteria for the selection of cloud services and the Service Level Agreement (SLA) management [38]. Afterwards, during cloud workflow run-time, service providers are obligated to complete workflow processes within those assigned temporal constraints; otherwise, a penalty may be enforced according to the service contracts signed. Therefore, the setting of high quality temporal constraints is very important to the successful completion of scientific cloud workflows.

In our temporal framework, the function of temporal constraint setting is realised through a three-step process. The first step is a forecasting process in which the workflow activity duration intervals are predicted by a time-series forecasting strategy. The second step is a win−win negotiation process between service users and service providers to specify the coarse-grained temporal constraints. The third step is a propagation process in which fine-grained temporal constraints are set automatically based on the results of the second step. The detailed process will be introduced in Section 4.2, and the algorithms for forecasting and setting will be further presented in Chapters 5 and 6, respectively.

The second component is temporal consistency monitoring, which deals with monitoring of temporal consistency state against temporal violations. Based on a temporal consistency model, the temporal consistency states of scientific cloud workflows should be under constant monitoring in order to detect potential temporal violations in a timely fashion. However, as mentioned before, the cost of temporal verification can be very huge due to the complexity and uncertainty in cloud workflow system environments. Therefore, cost-effective strategies need to be designed to detect potential temporal violations in an efficient fashion.

In our framework, the function of temporal consistency state monitoring is realised through a two-step process. The first step is temporal checkpoint selection. Given the probability-based temporal consistency model, our minimum probability time redundancy-based CSS can choose the minimal set of activity points (i.e. necessary and sufficient checkpoints) for temporal verification. The second process is temporal verification, which checks the current temporal consistency states at the selected checkpoints using our probability-based temporal consistency model. In our temporal framework, instead of the conventional four types of checkpoint and temporal consistency states, only one type of checkpoint and temporal consistency state (i.e. recoverable state) needs to be verified, thus reducing the cost of checkpoint selection and temporal verification. The detailed process will be introduced in Section 4.3, and the algorithms will be further presented in Chapter 7.

The third component is temporal violation handling, which deals with recovery of temporal violations. Based on the results of the previous component for monitoring temporal consistency, a necessary and sufficient checkpoint is selected where a potential temporal violation is detected. Conventional temporal verification work believes in the philosophy that temporal violation handling should be executed at all necessary and sufficient checkpoints. However, given the probability of self-recovery (i.e. the time deficit can be automatically compensated by the saved execution time of the subsequent workflow activities), we have identified that such a philosophy is not necessarily ideal. Therefore, a temporal violation handling point selection process should be designed to further determine whether temporal violation handling is necessary at each checkpoint. Here, the necessity for temporal violation handling points means that the probability of self-recovery (i.e. the time deficit can be automatically compensated by the saved execution time of the subsequent workflow segment) is below a certain threshold, i.e. the probability of temporal violations is high enough that temporal violation handling is necessary. If a temporal violation handling point is selected, then temporal violation handling strategies should be executed. In our temporal framework, we mainly focus on those statistically recoverable temporal violations which can be recovered by light-weight temporal violation handling strategies[1]. For such a purpose, representative metaheuristics-based workflow rescheduling strategies are investigated, adapted and implemented under a

---

[1] Statistically recoverable and non-recoverable temporal violations are defined in Section 7.2.1 and their corresponding light-weight and heavy-weight handling strategies are overviewed in Section 9.2.

novel general two-stage local workflow rescheduling strategy to handle temporal violations. Since our temporal violation handling strategy is fully automatic and utilises only existing system resources without recruiting additional ones, the cost of temporal violation handling can be significantly reduced compared with many conventional heavy-weight temporal violation handling strategies.

In our temporal framework, temporal violation handling is realised through a two-step process. The first step is an adaptive temporal violation handling point selection process. Motivated by software testing, a novel adaptive temporal violation handling point selection strategy is designed which can significantly reduce the overall cost of temporal violation handling while still maintaining satisfactory temporal QoS. In our strategy, a temporal violation handling point is selected only when the probability of self-recovery is below the adaptively adjusted threshold which denotes the requirement for temporal violation handling. After a temporal violation handling point is selected, corresponding handling strategies should be executed. In our framework, a novel temporal violation handling strategy is implemented which consists of three levels of temporal violations (level I, level II and level III temporal violations) and their corresponding handling strategies (*PTDA*, *ACOWR* and *PTDA + ACOWR*). Our temporal violation handling strategy is mainly based on *ACOWR*, an ACO-based two-stage local workflow rescheduling strategy, which attempts to compensate the time deficits with the reduced workflow execution time through optimising the workflow scheduling plan. Here, 'two-stage' means a two-stage searching process designed in our strategy to strike a balance between time-deficit compensation and the completion time of other activities while 'local' means the rescheduling of 'local' workflow segments with 'local' resources. To handle temporal violations, the key optimisation objective for workflow rescheduling is to maximise the compensation time. However, if we focus only on the speed-up of the workflow instances that have temporal violations, then the completion time of other activities, such as the segments of other workflow instances and ordinary non-workflow tasks, could be delayed and may violate temporal constraints of their own, if any. Therefore, a balance between time-deficit compensation and the completion time of other activities needs to be considered; otherwise, the overall efficiency of scientific cloud workflow systems will be significantly deteriorated. As for local rescheduling, it is designed for the requirement of cost-effectiveness. As stated previously, our temporal violation handling strategy utilises only existing resources that are currently deployed in the system instead of recruiting additional resources. Meanwhile, unlike global rescheduling, which modifies the global Task-Resource list for the entire workflow instance, our strategy focuses only on the local workflow segment and optimises the integrated Task-Resource list. The detailed process will be introduced in Section 4.4, and the algorithms will be further presented in Chapters 8 and 9.

4.2 Component I: Temporal Constraint Setting

Component I is temporal constraint setting. As depicted in Table 4.1, the input includes process models (cloud workflow process definitions) and system logs for

Table 4.1 Component I: Temporal Constraint Setting

Strategy overview	Input: process models and system logs for scientific cloud workflows
	Output: coarse-grained and fine-grained upper bound temporal constraints
	Methods: statistical time-series-pattern-based forecasting strategy; weighted joint normal distribution; probability-based temporal consistency model; win—win negotiation process; automatic propagation
Step 1: Forecasting activity duration intervals	Based on system logs, a statistical time-series-pattern-based forecasting strategy is applied for estimation of workflow activity duration intervals
Step 2: Setting coarse-grained temporal constraints	With the probability-based temporal consistency model, a win—win negotiation process between service users and service providers is designed to set coarse-grained temporal constraints. The negotiation process can be conducted in either a time- or probability-oriented way
Step 3: Setting fine-grained temporal constraints	Based on coarse-grained temporal constraints, fine-grained temporal constraints can be assigned through an automatic propagation process

scientific cloud workflows. The output includes both coarse-grained and fine-grained upper bound temporal constraints. Temporal constraints mainly include three types, i.e. upper bound, lower bound and fixed time. An upper bound constraint between two activities is a relative time value so that the duration between them must be less than or equal to it. As discussed in [21], conceptually, a lower bound constraint is symmetric to an upper bound constraint and a fixed-time constraint can be viewed as a special case of upper bound constraint, hence they can be treated similarly. Therefore, in this book, we focus only on upper bound constraints.

The first step is to forecast workflow activity duration intervals. Activity duration interval is one of the basic elements for the temporal consistency model. For workflow activities, the accuracy of their estimated durations is critical for the effectiveness of our temporal framework. However, forecasting is not a trivial issue in cloud workflow environments due to its complexity and uncertainty by nature. For such a purpose, a statistical time-series pattern-based forecasting strategy is designed. Unlike conventional strategies which build forecasting models based on several dominated affecting factors for activity durations (e.g. CPU load, network speed and memory space), our forecasting strategy focuses on the performance patterns of activity durations themselves and tries to predict an accurate interval based on the most similar historical time-series patterns. Details of the forecasting strategy will be presented in Chapter 5.

The second step is to set coarse-grained temporal constraints. Coarse-grained temporal constraints are those assigned for entire workflow instances (deadlines) and local workflow segments (milestones). They are usually specified by service users based on their own interests. However, as analysed in Section 2.3, to ensure the quality of temporal constraints, a balance should be considered between the service user's requirements and the system's performance. For such a purpose, with the probability-based temporal consistency model, a win—win negotiation process between service users and service providers is designed to support the setting of coarse-grained temporal constraints. The negotiation process can be conducted either in a time-oriented way where the service user suggests new temporal constraints and the service provider replies with the corresponding probability consistency state (i.e. probability confidence for completing the workflow instance within the specified temporal constraint) or in a probability-oriented way where the service user suggests new probability consistency state and the service provider replies with the corresponding temporal constraints. Finally, a set of balanced coarse-grained temporal constraints can be achieved. Details about the setting strategy for coarse-grained temporal constraints will be presented in Chapter 6.

The third step is to set fine-grained temporal constraints. Given the results of the previous step, coarse-grained temporal constraints need to be propagated along the entire workflow instance to assign fine-grained temporal constraints for each workflow activity. In our strategy, an automatic propagation process is designed to assign fine-grained temporal constraints based on their aggregated coarse-grained ones. A case study demonstrates that our setting strategy for fine-grained temporal constraints is very efficient and accurate. Details of the setting strategy for fine-grained temporal constraints will also be presented in Chapter 6.

4.3   Component II: Temporal Consistency Monitoring

Component II is temporal consistency monitoring. As depicted in Table 4.2, the input includes temporal constraints assigned by Component I at workflow build-time and run-time workflow activity durations for completed activities and predicted activity duration intervals for those not-yet-commenced activities (based on the forecasting strategy in Component I). The output is mainly on the current temporal consistency state at a selected activity point, i.e. checkpoint. The target of this component is to keep the cloud workflow execution under constant monitoring and detect potential temporal violations as early as possible.

The first step is to select temporal checkpoints. Since it is normally too expensive to conduct temporal verification at every activity point but insufficient to conduct temporal verification only at a few pre-defined activity points, the target of a CSS is to select only necessary and sufficient activity points where potential temporal violations are detected. Therefore, the cost of temporal verification will be minimised. In our framework, a minimum probability time redundancy-based CSS is designed for selecting only necessary and sufficient checkpoints given our probability-based temporal consistency model. Necessary and sufficient checkpoints serve as important bases for all the subsequent steps. Details of the CSS will be presented in Chapter 7.

Table 4.2 Component II: Temporal Consistency Monitoring

Strategy overview	Input: temporal constraints; run-time activity durations (for completed activities); predicted activity duration intervals (for non-commenced activities)
	Output: necessary and sufficient checkpoints; temporal consistency state and the level of temporal violation at a specific checkpoint; methods: probability-based temporal consistency model; minimum probability time redundancy-based checkpoint selection strategy; probability temporal consistency verification strategy
Step 1: Selecting temporal checkpoints	With the minimum probability time redundancy-based checkpoint selection strategy, only necessary and sufficient checkpoints are selected
Step 2: Verifying temporal consistency states	With the probability-based temporal consistency model, temporal verification is conducted at each checkpoint to verify the current temporal consistency state and determine the level of temporal violation to facilitate temporal violation handling

The second step is temporal verification. Temporal verification verifies the current temporal consistency state so as to determine whether a temporal violation takes place and/or the level of current temporal violations. Given a specific temporal consistency model which may define different types of temporal consistency states, conventional temporal verification may need to be conducted several times to identify the current temporal consistency states. For example, in the conventional multi-states-based temporal consistency model, if the current temporal consistency state is strong inconsistency, then the temporal verification process may be conducted three times, i.e. starting from the verification of strong consistency, then weak consistency, then weak inconsistency, before the verification of strong inconsistency [16]. Therefore, the cost of another three instances of temporal verification is actually unnecessary and should be avoided. In our strategy, with the probability-based temporal consistency model where continuous temporal consistency states are defined, it is no longer necessary to verify different types of temporal consistency states as one is sufficient to determine the actual level of temporal violations. Specifically, each temporal consistency state is associated with a unique probability value and is within the range of either statistically recoverable or non-recoverable temporal violations. Therefore, checkpoint selection and temporal verification are required to be conducted only once at every activity. Details of the temporal verification strategy will be presented in Chapter 7.

4.4 Component III: Temporal Violation Handling

The third component is temporal violation handling. At a selected temporal violation handling point, temporal violation handling tackles the existing temporal violations by reducing or, ideally, removing the occurred time deficits. As depicted in

Table 4.3 Component III: Temporal Violation Handling

Strategy overview	Input: necessary and sufficient checkpoints; temporal consistency states; workflow scheduling plans
	Output: violation handling points; regenerated workflow scheduling plans
	Methods: adaptive violation handing point selection strategy; violation handling strategy (take $PTDA + ACOWR$ as an example)
Step 1: Selecting temporal violation handling points	Based on the adaptive violation handling point selection strategy, a subset of checkpoints selected in Step 1 is further selected as the set of violation handling points for further handling
Step 2: Temporal violation handling	$PTDA + ACOWR$
Step 2.1: allocating probability time deficit	Based on a probability time-deficit allocation strategy, allocating the probability time deficit to workflow activities in the subsequent local workflow segment
Step 2.2: generating integrated task-VM list	Generating an integrated Task-VM list which represents the current scheduling plan of workflow activities in the subsequent local workflow segment and their co-allocated activities
Step 2.3: optimising workflow local scheduling plan	Based on the probability time deficit allocated in Step 2.1 and the integrated Task-VM list obtained in Step 2.2, the ACO-based two-stage workflow local rescheduling strategy utilises the metaheuristics-based scheduling algorithms to generate new workflow scheduling plan for recovering the detected temporal violation

Table 4.3, the input includes the necessary and sufficient checkpoints, temporal consistency states and the current workflow scheduling plans (which define the assignment of workflow activities to computing resources, e.g. virtual machines in cloud computing environments). The output includes the temporal violation handling points and regenerated workflow scheduling plans which can reduce or, ideally, remove the occurred time deficits of violated workflow instances.

The first step is to select temporal violation handling points. In the conventional temporal verification work [16,18,67], a temporal violation handling point is regarded as similar to a necessary and sufficient checkpoint in nature, i.e. temporal violation handling should be triggered whenever a temporal violation is detected. However, due to the dynamic nature of cloud workflow environments, the number of selected checkpoints can still be huge, especially in large-scale scientific cloud workflow applications. Therefore, given the probability of self-recovery and motivated by random testing techniques, an adaptive temporal violation handling point selection strategy is designed to further select a subset of necessary and sufficient checkpoints for temporal violation handling. Those temporal violation handling points are selected when the probability of self-recovery is below the adaptively adjusted threshold which indicates the necessity for temporal violation handling. Details of the temporal violation handling point selection strategy will be presented in Chapter 8.

The second step is the execution of a temporal violation handling strategy at the selected handling point. As will be introduced in Section 9.4, in our temporal framework, three temporal violation handling strategies are employed to tackle three levels of temporal violations, namely *PTDA* for level I temporal violations, *ACOWR* for level II temporal violations and *PTDA + ACOWR* for level III temporal violations. Here, in Table 4.3, we take *PTDA + ACOWR* as an example to introduce the temporal violation handling process. The details of these strategies will be presented in Chapter 9.

For *PTDA + ACOWR*, Step 2.1 is to allocate probability time deficit. Based on *PTDA*, the occurred time deficit is allocated proportionally to the workflow activities of the subsequent local workflow segment. The purpose of time-deficit allocation is to ensure the balance among the subsequent workflow activities to share the time deficit. Unlike the conventional strategy, which assigns the time deficit to all the workflow activities remained in the workflow instance [18], our strategy considers only the subsequent local workflow segment after the selected handling point. Therefore, the number of workflow activities involved in the workflow rescheduling process is significantly reduced and thus can save the temporal violation handling cost.

Step 2.2 is to generate an integrated Task-VM list. The integrated Task-VM list represents the current scheduling plan for the activities in the local workflow segment and their co-allocated tasks. Since the rescheduling of workflow activities in the local workflow segment will change not only their own task assignment but also inevitably that of other co-allocated tasks, if we do not consider the other co-allocated tasks, their execution time will probably be delayed and may even violate their own temporal constraints, if any. The purpose of the integrated Task-VM list is to consider all the tasks and virtual machines that will be affected in the rescheduling process. In such a case, a balance between the time compensation of violated workflow instances and the overall efficiency of the cloud workflow system could be achieved. Details of the integrated Task-VM list will also be presented in Section 9.3.1.

Step 2.3 is to optimise the workflow local scheduling plan. The target of the optimisation process is to reduce the execution time of the activities in the local workflow segment so that the time deficit can be compensated. In our two-stage workflow local rescheduling strategy, there are two searching processes. The first searching process is a metaheuristics-based searching process in which the overall makespan and cost for the integrated Task-VM list are optimised. Here, two representative metaheuristics including GA and ACO are investigated. As for the second searching process, selected valid candidates (scheduling plans) are compared in order to find the best solution in which the execution time of the local workflow segment is minimal, i.e. the solution that can compensate the occurred time deficit as much as possible, or even remove it entirely. Based on such a two-stage searching process, the balance between the execution of workflow instances with temporal violations and those without temporal violations can be achieved.

Component I

Temporal Constraint Setting

5 Forecasting Scientific Cloud Workflow Activity Duration Intervals

As discussed in Chapter 2, workflow activity duration is one of the basic elements in the temporal consistency model, and thus its accuracy is critical for the effectiveness of temporal verification and all the other related components such as temporal checkpoint selection and temporal violation handling. Therefore, an accurate forecasting strategy is required to predict cloud workflow activity durations. However, it is not a trivial issue due to the dynamic nature of cloud computing environments. In this chapter, we present a statistical time-series-based forecasting strategy for scientific cloud workflow activity duration intervals. The comparison results demonstrate that our strategy has better performance than the other existing representative strategies.

This chapter is organised as follows. Section 5.1 gives a general introduction about cloud workflow activity durations. Section 5.2 presents the specifically related work and problem analysis. Section 5.3 presents the novel statistical time-series-pattern-based forecasting strategy. Section 5.4 demonstrates the experimental results.

This chapter is mainly based on our work presented in Refs [59,65].

5.1 Cloud Workflow Activity Durations

Due to the dynamic nature of cloud computing environments, it is a critical yet challenging issue to maintain high temporal QoS in cloud workflow systems. The foundation for workflow temporal verification is the temporal consistency model

Temporal QoS Management in Scientific Cloud Workflow Systems. DOI: 10.1016/B978-0-12-397010-7.00005-7

which consists of three basic elements including temporal constraints, real activity durations of completed workflow activities and the estimated activity durations of not-yet-commenced workflow activities. Among them, temporal constraints are specified at build time and normally remain unchanged at run-time. As for real activity durations of completed workflow activities, they can be easily obtained at run-time. However, the estimated activity durations of uncompleted workflow activities are required both at build time for modelling tasks such as constraint setting and at run-time for monitoring tasks such as temporal verification. Therefore, the accuracy of the estimated activity durations is very important for supporting temporal QoS in scientific cloud workflow systems.

Interval forecasting for activity durations is to estimate the upper bound and the lower bound of activity durations. Since the accurate point prediction of activity duration is very difficult in dynamic system environments, the practical way is to estimate the activity duration intervals [14]. Moreover, a lot of workflow management tasks such as load balancing and workflow scheduling need the data on the upper bound and the lower bound of activity durations in order to make various decisions. Therefore, effective interval forecasting strategies need to be investigated for scientific cloud workflow systems. However, it is a non-trivial issue. On one hand, scientific cloud workflow activity durations consist of complex components. In workflows, activity duration covers the time interval from the initial submission to the final completion of a workflow activity. Hence, besides the exact execution time on allocated resources, they also consist of extra time, i.e. workflow overheads. According to [77], there exist four main categories of workflow overheads in scientific applications including middleware overhead, data transfer overhead, loss of parallelism overhead and activity-related overhead. Similar overheads also exist in scientific cloud workflow systems. In scientific cloud workflows, activity durations involve many more affecting factors than the execution time of conventional computation tasks which are dominated by the load of high-performance computing resources. On the other hand, the service performance is highly dynamic. Scientific cloud workflows are deployed on cloud computing infrastructures where the performance of cloud service is highly dynamic since they are organised and managed in a heterogeneous and loosely coupled fashion. Moreover, the workload of these shared resources, such as the computing units, the storage spaces and the network, keeps changing dynamically. Therefore, many traditional multivariate models which consist of many affecting factors such as CPU load, memory space and network speed [34,98,108,109] are either unsatisfactory in performance or too complex to be applicable in practice, let alone the fact that it is very difficult, if not impossible, to measure these affecting factors in the distributed and heterogeneous computing environments such as cloud and grid [35,44]. There are also many strategies which define a type of 'templates' like models [73,74]. These models may include workflow activity properties such as workflow structural properties (like control and data flow dependency, etc.), activity properties (like problem size, executable, versions, etc.), execution properties (like scheduling algorithm, external load, number of CPUs, number of jobs in the queue, free memory, etc.), and then use 'similarity search' to find out the most similar activity instances and predict activity durations [73]. However, they also suffer the same problems faced by traditional multivariate models mentioned above.

In this book, we focus on data- and computation-intensive scientific cloud workflows. In scientific cloud workflows, workflow activities normally occupy some fixed resources and run continuously for a long time due to their own computation complexity – e.g. the activities for generating large number of de-dispersion files and the running of seeking algorithms in the pulsar searching scientific workflow described in Section 1.2.1. The execution time of a data-/computation-intensive activity is mainly decided by the average performance of the workflow system over its lifecycle. Therefore, it is important that the forecasting strategy in a cloud workflow system can effectively meet these criteria.

5.2 Related Work and Problem Analysis

5.2.1 Related Work

In this book, we focus on time-series-based interval forecasting strategies. Five service performance estimation approaches, including simulation, analytical modelling, historical data, online learning and hybrid, are presented in Ref. [103]. In general, time-series forecasting belongs to historical data-based approaches. Currently, much work utilises multivariate models and focuses on the prediction of CPU load since it is the dominant factor for the durations of computation-intensive activities. Typical linear time-series models such as AR, MA and Box-Jenkins are fitted to perform host load prediction in Ref. [34] where it claims that most time-series models are sufficient for host load prediction and recommends AR(16) which consumes miniscule computation cost. The work in Ref. [57] presents a one-step-ahead and low-overhead time-series forecasting strategy which tracks recent trends by giving more weight to recent data. A hybrid model which integrates the AR model with confidence interval is presented in Ref. [102] to perform n-step-ahead load prediction. A different strategy presented in Ref. [90] predicts application duration with historical information where search techniques are employed to determine those application characteristics that yield the best definition of similarity. The work in Ref. [4] investigates extended forecasting of both CPU and network load on computation grid to achieve effective load balancing. The authors in Ref. [102] mention the problem of turning points which causes large prediction errors in time-series models. However, few solutions have been presented to investigate more affecting factors and handle turning points. Different from the above work, there are a few literatures that utilise univariate models. NWS [98] implements three types of univariate time-series forecasting methods including mean-based, median-based and autoregressive methods, and dynamically chooses the one exhibiting the lowest cumulative error measure at any given moment to generate a forecast. Hence, NWS automatically identifies the best forecasting methods for any given resource. The work in Ref. [35] presents a Dynamic Exponential Smoothing (DES) method which forecasts the future duration based only on its past values.

The basic motivation for DES is to handle the problems of sudden peaks and level switches. DES computes the optimal parameter for different classes of fluctuations, and it can consistently outperform the common prediction methods, such as the NWS predictor, AR(16) and ES [35] in a grid environment. However, to the best of our knowledge, no existing work has been presented so far to effectively address the forecasting of activity durations in scientific cloud workflow systems.

Time-series patterns are those time-series segments which have high probability to repeat themselves (similar in the overall shape but maybe with different amplitudes and/or durations) in a large time-series data set [14,43,49,59]. Time-series patterns can be employed for complex prediction tasks, such as trend analysis and value estimation in stock markets, product sales and weather forecasts [47]. The two major tasks in pattern-based time-series forecasting are pattern recognition, which discovers time-series patterns according to the pattern definition, and pattern matching, which searches for similar patterns with given query sequences. To facilitate complex time-series analysis such as time-series clustering and fast similarity search, time-series segmentation is often employed to reduce the variances in each segment so that they can be described by simple linear or non-linear models [53]. In general, most segmentation algorithms can be classified into three generic algorithms with some variations, namely Sliding Windows, Top-Down and Bottom-Up [53]. The process of Sliding Windows is like sequential scanning where the segments keep increasing with each new point until some thresholds are violated. The basic idea of the Top-Down algorithm is the repetition of the splitting process where the original time series is equally divided until all segments meet the stopping criteria. In contrast to Top-Down, the basic process of the Bottom-Up algorithm is merging: the finest segments are merged continuously until some thresholds are violated. The main problem for Sliding Windows is that it can only 'look forward' but not 'look backward'. The main problem for Top-Down is that it lacks the ability to merge, while the main problem for Bottom-Up is that it lacks the ability to split. Therefore, hybrid algorithms, which take advantage of the three generic algorithms by modifications and combinations, are often more preferable in practice [47,53,59,94].

5.2.2 Problem Analysis

In cloud workflow systems, most workflow activities are data and/or computation intensive and, as such, require constant processing of specific resources such as network, I/O facility and computing units for a long period of time. For workflow activities in data-/computation-intensive scientific applications, two problems of their duration series are limited sample size and frequent turning points. These two problems are very common in most scientific applications. Therefore, an effective forecasting strategy is required to tackle these two problems, which are explained as follows.

1. Limited sample size. Current work on the prediction of CPU load such as AR(16) demands a large sample size to fit the model and at least 16 prior points to make one

prediction. However, this becomes a real issue for scientific workflow activity duration series. Unlike CPU load, which reflects an instant state and in which the observations can be measured at any time with high sampling rates such as 1 Hz [108], scientific workflow activity durations denote discrete long-term intervals since activity instances occur less frequently and take minutes or even hours to be completed. Meanwhile, due to the heavy workload brought about by these activities and the limits of available underlying resources (given requirements on the capability and performance), the number of concurrent activity instances is usually constrained in the systems. Therefore, the duration sample size is often limited and linear time-series models cannot be fitted effectively.

2. Frequent turning points. A serious problem, which deteriorates the effectiveness of linear time-series models, is the frequent occurrence of turning points where large deviations from the previous duration sequences take place [108]. This problem resides not only in the prediction of CPU load but also in the forecasting of activity durations as observed and discussed in much of the literature [36,108]. Actually, due to the large durations and the uneven distribution of activity instances, the states of the underlying system environment usually differ greatly even between neighbouring duration-series segments. For example, the average number of concurrent activity instances in the observation unit of (10:00 a.m.−11:00 a.m.) may well be bigger than that of (9:00 a.m.−10:00 a.m.) due to the normal schedule of working hours. Therefore, activity instances are unevenly distributed and frequent turning points are hence often expected. This further emphasises the importance of effective discovery and handling of turning points in the forecasting of scientific workflow activity durations.

In this chapter, to address the above issues, we present a statistical time-series-pattern-based forecasting strategy which can achieve better performance and maintain it more consistently in the interval forecasting of activity durations in cloud workflow systems.

5.3   Statistical Time-Series-Pattern-Based Forecasting Strategy

In this chapter, we utilise time-series-based forecasting models. Time-series models are probably the most widely used statistical ways for formulating and forecasting the dynamic behaviour of complex objects [14,59]. A time series is a set of observations made sequentially through time. Some representative time series, including marketing time series, temperature time series and quality control time series, are effectively applied in various scientific and business domains [49]. Similarly, a cloud workflow activity duration time series, or duration series for short, is composed of ordered duration samples obtained from cloud workflow system logs or other forms of historical data. Therefore, duration series is a specific type of time series in the cloud workflow domain. In this book, the term 'time series' and 'duration series' can be used interchangeably in most cases. Current forecasting strategies for computation tasks mainly reside on the prediction of CPU load [4,108]. However, this is quite different from the prediction of cloud workflow activity durations due to the reasons mentioned earlier.

In this chapter, instead of applying traditional multivariate models, we conduct univariate time-series analysis which analyses the behaviour of a duration series to build a model for the correlation between its neighbouring samples — in other words, forecasting the future activity durations based only on the past activity durations [14]. Specifically, a novel non-linear time-series segmentation algorithm named $K-MaxSDev$ is presented to facilitate a statistical time-series-pattern-based forecasting strategy. Two problems of the duration series which seriously hinder the effectiveness of conventional time-series forecasting strategies are limited sample size and frequent turning points. Limited sample size impedes the fitting of time-series models and frequent turning points where dramatic deviations take place significantly deteriorate the overall accuracy of time-series forecasting. To address these two problems, we utilise a statistical time-series-pattern-based forecasting strategy. First, an effective periodical sampling plan is conducted to build a representative duration series. Second, a pattern recognition process employs our $K-MaxSDev$ time-series segmentation algorithm to discover the minimum number of potential patterns which are further validated and associated with specified turning points. Third, given the latest duration sequences, pattern matching and interval forecasting are performed to make predictions based on the statistical features of the best-matched patterns. Meanwhile, concerning the occurrences of turning points, three types of duration sequences are identified and then handled with different pattern matching results.

The simulation experiments conducted in our SwinDeW-C cloud workflow system demonstrate that our time-series segmentation algorithm is capable of discovering the smallest potential pattern set compared with three generic algorithms, i.e. Sliding Windows, Top-Down and Bottom-Up [53]. The comparison results further demonstrate that our statistical time-series-pattern-based strategy behaves better than several representative time-series forecasting strategies, namely MEAN [34], LAST [35], Exponential Smoothing (ES) [35], Moving Average (MA) [14], AutoRegression (AR) [14] and Network Weather Service (NWS) [98], in the prediction of high-confidence duration intervals and the handling of turning points.

5.3.1 Statistical Time-Series Patterns

The motivation for pattern-based time-series forecasting comes from the observation that for those duration-series segments where the number of concurrent activity instances is similar, these activity durations reveal comparable statistical features. It is obvious that when the number of concurrent activities increases, the average resources that can be scheduled for each activity decrease while the overall workflow overheads increase and vice versa. Similar observation is reported in Ref. [36] between the task execution time and the resource load in a global-scale (grid) environment. Accordingly, the duration series behaves up and down though it may not necessarily follow a linear relationship. This phenomenon is especially evident when, for example, workflow systems adopt market-driven or trust-driven resource management strategies that give preference to a limited range of resources [11]. Furthermore, if these segments reappear frequently during a duration series, they can be deemed potential patterns which represent unique behaviour of the duration series under certain circumstances. Therefore, if we are able to define and discover these typical patterns, the intervals of future durations can be estimated with the statistical features of the closest patterns by matching the latest duration sequences. Based on this motivation, we present here the definition of our statistical time-series patterns as follows.

Definition 5.1. (Statistical Time-Series Patterns): For a specific time series $T = \{X_1, X_2, \ldots, X_n\}$ which consists of n observations, its pattern set is *Patterns* = $\{P_1, P_2, \ldots, P_m\}$ where $\sum_{i=1}^{m} \text{length}(P_i) \leq n$. For pattern P_i of length k, it is a reoccurred segment which has unique statistical features of sample mean μ and sample standard deviation σ, where $\mu = \sum_{i=1}^{k} X_i/k$ and $\sigma = \sqrt{\left(\sum_{i=1}^{k}(X_i - \mu)\right)^2 /(k-1)}$.

Note that in this chapter, since we use statistical features to describe the behaviour of each time-series segment in an overall sense, the order of patterns is important for time-series forecasting, while the order of sample points within each pattern is not. Meanwhile, for the purpose of generality, sample mean and standard deviation are employed as two basic statistical features to formulate each pattern. However, other criteria such as the median value, the trend and the length of each segment (the number of samples it consists of) can also be considered to make fine-grained definitions.

5.3.2 Strategy Overview

As depicted in the outlier of Figure 5.1, our statistical time-series-pattern-based forecasting strategy consists of four major steps which are duration-series building, duration pattern recognition, duration pattern matching and duration interval forecasting. The inner three circles stand for the three basic factors concerned with

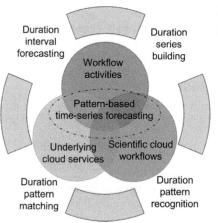

Figure 5.1 Overview of statistical time-series-pattern-based forecasting strategy.

activity durations: characteristics of the workflow activities, specifications of scientific cloud workflows and performance of cloud services.

Here, we illustrate the process of each step while leaving the detailed algorithms to Sections 5.3.3 and 5.3.4.

1. *Duration-series building*: It is designed to tackle the problem of limited sample size. Building duration series is actually a sampling process in which the historical durations for a specific activity are sampled at equal observation units from cloud workflow system logs or other historical data sources and are then arranged according to the order of their submission time. In our strategy, we adopt a periodical sampling plan in which the samples having their submission time belonging to the same observation unit of each period are treated as samples for the same unit. Afterwards, a representative duration series is built with the sample mean of each unit. This periodical sampling plan effectively solves the problem of limited sample size and uneven distribution since samples are assembled to increase the density of each observation unit. Meanwhile, recurrent frequencies of duration-series segments are statistically guaranteed. Therefore, we only need to analyse the representative duration series, and if a pattern is identified for this representative duration series, it is also statistically a pattern for the whole historical duration series. Note that there are many existing techniques to determine the specific value of the period [15,54], and it is strongly dependent on the real world situation of the cloud workflow system. However, it can also be estimated by system managers from the main source of system workload. For example, in many cloud workflow systems — especially those that mainly deal with complex data-/computation-intensive scientific processes such as weather forecasts and pulsar searching by a specific group of users — the system workload normally behaves periodically according to the lifecycle of these workflow processes. Specifically, if these processes are conducted routinely, say once every day, the system workload probably also behaves similarly with a period of one day in a rough sense. Therefore, the value of the period can first be chosen as one day and adjusted according to historical data.

2. *Duration pattern recognition*: Duration pattern recognition is to discover duration-series patterns by an effective pattern recognition process. The pattern recognition process contains two steps: time-series segmentation and pattern validation. The first step is to identify a potential pattern set. For this purpose, we design a novel non-linear time-series segmentation algorithm named $K-MaxSDev$ to achieve better performance in the discovery of the potential duration-series patterns compared with three generic algorithms. These duration-series patterns reflect the fundamental behaviour patterns of duration series. The second step is to check the validity of these segments by the minimum length threshold and specify the turning points for each valid pattern. The minimum length threshold is set to filter those segments that do not have enough samples to make effective pattern matching. Meanwhile, we emphasise the proactive identification of turning points so as to eliminate large prediction errors. In our strategy, turning points are defined as those on the edge of two adjacent segments where the testing criterion is violated.

3. *Duration pattern matching*: Given the latest duration sequence, duration pattern matching is to find out the closest pattern with similarity search. The latest duration sequence is compared with valid duration-series patterns obtained through pattern recognition. Moreover, due to the occurrences of turning points, three types of duration sequences, including the type where the sequence contains internal turning points, the type where the next value of the sequence is probably a turning point and the type for the remainder of

the sequences, are first identified and then specified with different means and standard deviations. Here, the distance in similarity search between two sequences is defined as the absolute differences of their sample means.

4. *Duration interval forecasting*: With the pattern matching results (the estimated mean value and associated turning points), duration intervals are specified accordingly with a given confidence under the assumption that the samples within a pattern follow the normal distribution [54].

This section briefly describes the process of our statistical time-series-pattern-based forecasting strategy. The technical details will be illustrated in the subsequent sections.

5.3.3   Novel Time-Series Segmentation Algorithm: K−MaxSDev

In this section, we present $K-MaxSDev$, a non-linear time-series segmentation algorithm which is designed to formulate the duration series with minimal number of segments, i.e. potential duration-series patterns. Here, K is the initial value for equal segmentation and $MaxSDev$ is the Maximum Standard Deviation specified as the testing criterion. The intuition for the initial K equal segmentation is an efficiency enhancement to the generic Bottom-Up algorithm which normally starts from the finest equal segments with the length of 2. We modify the initial equal segments with a moderately larger K which can be either user specified or with the empirical function presented later in this section. This modification can save significant computation time at the initial stage. $MaxSDev$ comes directly from the requirement for precise interval forecasting where the variances in each segment need to be controlled within a maximum threshold in order to guarantee an accurate small bound of the predicted durations, i.e. the duration intervals.

The notations and the pseudo-code for the $K-MaxSDev$ algorithm are presented in Tables 5.1 and 5.2, respectively. $K-MaxSDev$ is a hybrid algorithm which can be described as follows. It starts from Bottom-Up with K initial equal segmentation, followed by the repetitive process of Sliding Windows and Top-Down with the testing criterion of $MaxSDev$. Here, the basic merging element of Sliding Windows is not a single point but a segment. Meanwhile, the windows can slide both forward and backward to merge as many segments as possible. As for Top-Down, it equally splits those segments which cannot be merged with any neighbours. This repetitive process stops when either the maximum repetition time R is

Table 5.1 Notations Used in $K-MaxSDev$

Seg_j	The jth segment of time series
$SDev(Seg_p, Seg_q)$	The standard deviation of all the samples in the pth and qth segments
Initial Seg(K)	The initial K equal segmentation for time series
Split(Seg_j)	Split the jth segment into two equal parts
Merge(Seg_p, Seg_q)	Merge the pth and qth segments
Delete(Seg_j)	Delete the jth segment

Table 5.2 Algorithm 1: $K-MaxSDev$ Time-Series Segmentation

Algorithm: K-MaxSDev
Input: Duration series T={$X_1, X_2, X_3 \ldots X_n$}, Const K, Const MaxSDev
Output: Segmented duration series D={$Seg_1, Seg_2, Seg_3 \ldots Seg_m$}

InitialSeg(K);   //Bottom-Up
Do
   for (j = 2, j ≤ K − 1, j++)
       if SDev(Seg_{j-1}, Seg_j) ≤ MaxSDev   //Sliding Windows-Backward
         Seg_j = Merge(Seg_{j-1}, Seg_j);
         Delete(Seg_{j-1}); K = K − 1; Update the index;
       end
       if SDev(Seg_j, Seg_{j+1}) ≤ MaxSDev   //Sliding Windows-Forward
         Seg_{j+1} = Merge(Seg_j, Seg_{j+1});
         Delete(Seg_j); K = K − 1; Update the index;
       end
       if SDev(Seg_{j-1}, Seg_j) > MaxSDev and SDev(Seg_j, Seg_{j+1}) > MaxSDev
         Split(Seg_j); K = K + 1; Update the index;   //Top-Down
       end
   end
Until (no individual segments can be merged with their neighbours)

---

reached or all individual segments can no longer be merged with their neighbours. Since the condition of 'all individual segments can no longer be merged with their neighbours' requires additional programming (or memory space) to store the segmentation results of the previous repetition, in practice, setting a maximum repetition time is a more efficient way to stop the repetition process. Meanwhile, the maximum repetition time can prevent the occurrence of endless loop (e.g. the deadlock of *Split* and *Merge*). According to our experiments, for most duration series the repetition process (i.e. the do-until part as shown in Algorithm 1 in Table 5.2) will be repeated no more than 3 times in most cases. Therefore, the maximum repetition time R is set as 5 in this chapter (including the experiments demonstrated in Section 5.4) but may be changed according to different system environments. Evidently, the aim here is to discover the minimum number of segments. The purpose of designing $K-MaxSDev$ rather than employing existing algorithms is to take full advantage of these three generic algorithms to achieve a better performance. Specifically, *Split* is to divide the current segment into two equal parts. In the case where the current segment has odd number of sample points, the point at the middle position will be included into the left segment. For example, if we *Split* a segment of {$p_2^1, p_2^2, p_2^3, p_2^4, p_2^5, p_2^6, p_2^7$}, it then becomes {$p_2^1, p_2^2, p_2^3, p_2^4, p_3^1, p_3^2, p_3^3$}. Its subsequent sample needs to update its index accordingly. *Merge* is to merge two neighbouring segments into one. For example, if we *Merge* two segments of {p_3^1, p_3^2, p_3^3} and {p_4^1, p_4^2}, it then becomes {$p_3^1, p_3^2, p_3^3, p_3^4, p_3^5$}. Its subsequent sample needs to update its index accordingly. *Delete* is to 'delete' the previous segment after *Merge*, i.e. update the index of the sample points. Like in the above *Merge* operation, the fourth segment is deleted, i.e. the previous fifth segment now becomes the new fourth segment and so on for the subsequent segments in the time series.

The empirical function for choosing K is based on the equal segmentation tests. The candidates of K are defined to be in the form of $2i$ and should be a value of no bigger than $n/4$ where i is a natural number and n is the length of the duration series. Otherwise, $K-MaxSDev$ turns into Bottom-Up with low efficiency. The process is that we first choose some of the candidates and perform equal segmentation. We calculate the mean for each segment and rank each candidate according to the average of the absolute differences between the means of neighbouring segments. The intuition is that initial segmentation should ensure large differences between the means of segments, so as to guarantee the efficiency of the segmentation algorithm. The formula for the empirical function is denoted as:

$$\text{Rank}(k) = \frac{\sum_{i=1}^{k-1} |\text{Mean}_{i+1} - \text{Mean}_i|}{k-1} \tag{5.1}$$

The theoretical basis for $MaxSDev$ is Tchebysheff's theorem [92] which has been widely used in statistics theory. According to the theorem, given a number d greater than or equal to 1 and a set of n samples, at least $[1 - (1/d)^2]$ of the samples will lie within d standard deviations of their mean, no matter what the actual probability distribution is. For example, 88.89% of the samples will fall into the interval of $(\mu - 3\sigma, \mu + 3\sigma)$. The value of μ and σ can be estimated by the sample mean and sample standard deviation as $\mu = \sum_{i=1}^{k} X_i/k$ and $\sigma = \sqrt{\left(\sum_{i=1}^{k}(X_i - \mu)\right)^2/(k-1)}$, respectively. If it happens to be a normal distribution, Tchebysheff's theorem turns to one of its special cases, i.e. the '3σ' rule which means with a probability of 99.73% that the sample is falling into the interval of $(\mu - 3\sigma, \mu + 3\sigma)$ [54]. Therefore, if we control the deviation to be less than $m\%$ of the mean, then $3\sigma \leq m\% \times \mu$ is ensured. We can thus specify $MaxSDev$ by:

$$MaxSDev = \frac{m\%}{3} \times \mu \tag{5.2}$$

$K-MaxSDev$ is the core algorithm for pattern recognition in our strategy, and it is applied to discover the minimal set of potential duration-series patterns.

5.3.4 Forecasting Algorithms

As presented in Section 5.3.2, the interval forecasting strategy for workflow activities in data-/computation-intensive scientific applications are composed of four major steps: duration-series building, duration pattern recognition, duration pattern matching and duration interval forecasting. In this section, we will present the detailed algorithms for each step. Note that since pattern matching and interval forecasting are always performed together, we illustrate them within an integrated process.

1. *Duration-series building*: As mentioned in Section 5.3.2, building the representative duration series is to address the problem of limited sample size. The representative duration series is built with a periodical sampling plan where the samples having their submission time belonging to the same observation unit of each period are treated as samples for the same unit. Afterwards, a representative duration series is built with the sample mean of each unit. The pseudo-code for the algorithm is presented in Table 5.3 (Algorithm 2). Here, the specific value of the period can be either user defined or obtained by existing techniques.

2. *Duration pattern recognition*: The duration pattern recognition process consists of two steps: time-series segmentation and pattern validation. The time-series segmentation step is to discover the minimal set of potential patterns with our novel $K-MaxSDev$ non-linear time-series segmentation algorithm as presented in Section 5.3.3. Therefore, its pseudo-code is omitted here. The pseudo-code for the second step of pattern validation together with turning points discovery is presented in Table 5.4 (Algorithm 3). With the segmented duration series, namely the discovered potential duration-series patterns, we further check their validity with the specified minimum length threshold defined as *Min_pattern_length*, which should be normally larger than 3 in order to get effective statistics for pattern matching and interval forecasting. Afterwards, we identify those turning points associated with each valid pattern. Specifically, turning points are defined as the points where the testing criterion of *MaxSDev* is violated. Since our $K-MaxSDev$ segmentation algorithm actually ensures that the violations of *MaxSDev* only occur on the edge of two adjacent segments, as shown in Table 5.4, turning points are specified by either the mean of the next invalid pattern or the first value of the next valid pattern. Evidently, this specification of turning points captures the locations where large prediction errors mostly tend to happen.

3. *Pattern matching and interval forecasting*: The most important issue for pattern matching and interval forecasting is to identify the type of the given latest duration sequence. Specifically, three types of duration sequences are defined in this chapter including the type where the sequence contains internal turning points, the type where the next value of the sequence is probably a turning point and the type for the remainder of the sequences. As presented in Table 5.5 (Algorithm 4), the types of sequences are identified based on standard deviations.

The first type of duration sequence has a standard deviation larger than *MaxSDev*; it cannot be matched with any valid patterns and must contain at least

Table 5.3 Algorithm 2: Representative Time-Series Building

Input: m Duration series $t^i = \{x_1^i, x_2^i, x_3^i \ldots x_n^i\}$ with the same length of a period
Output: Representative Time Series $T = \{X_1, X_2, X_3 \ldots X_n\}$

While not end of the time series
  for (j = 1, j ≤ m, j++)
    for (k = 1, j ≤ n, k++)

$$X_k = \frac{\sum_{i=1}^{m} x_k^j}{m}$$

    end
  end
end

Table 5.4 Algorithm 3: Pattern Validation and Turning Points Discovery

Input: Segmented duration series D = {Seg_1, Seg_2 ... Seg_m}, Const Min_pattern_length
Output: Duration patterns Pattern[ ] and associated turning points

Pattern[ ] = { };
  for (i = 1, i ≤ D.length, i++)   // Checking Patterns
    Pattern[i] = Seg_i;
    Pattern[i].mean = Seg_i.mean; Pattern[i].sdev = Seg_i.sdev;
    if Seg_i.length < Min_pattern_length
      Pattern[i].valid = false;
    else
      Pattern[i].valid = true;
    end
  end
  for (j = 1, j ≤ Pattern.length, j++)   // Specifying Turning Points
    if Pattern[i].valid = true
      if Pattern[i + 1].valid = true
        Pattern[i].turningpoint = Pattern[i + 1].firstvalue
      else
        Pattern[i].turningpoint = Pattern[i +1].mean
      end
    end
  end

Table 5.5 Algorithm 4: Pattern Matching and Duration Interval Forecasting

Input: Latest duration sequence DS, Duration patterns Pattern[], Const ms = MaxSDev,
      Const Min_pattern_length, Const λ (α% confidence percentile)
Output: Matched pattern MP and duration interval DI(min, max)

  if DS.sdev ≥ ms   // The latest duration sequence contains turning point in itself
    While (DS.sdev ≥ ms) // remove the part before and include the turning point
      DS = DS − DS.firstvalue;
    end
    DI(min, max) = (DS.mean − λ *ms, DS.mean + λ *ms);
  else   // λ is the α% confidence percentile for normal distribution
    if DS.length ≥ Min_pattern_length   // ensure a valid pattern matching
      MP = Min (Abs(Pattern.mean − DS.mean))
      // Min( ) returns the pattern with minimum absolute difference of mean
      if MP.sdev < DS.sdev < ms
        // The next value is highly possible to be a turning point
        DI(min, max) = (MP.turningpoint − λ *ms, MP.turningpoint + λ *ms);
      else if DS.sdev ≤ MP.sdev
        DI(min, max) = (MP.mean − λ *MP.sdev, MP.mean + λ *MP.sdev)
      end
    else // Sample size is too small to match a valid pattern
      DI(min, max) = (DS.mean − A *ms, DS.mean + A *ms);
    end
  end

one turning point. Therefore, we need to first locate the turning points and then conduct pattern matching with the remainder of the duration sequence. However, to ensure the effectiveness of the prediction, if the length of the remaining duration sequence is smaller than the minimum pattern length, the duration interval is specified with the mean of the duration sequence, while its standard deviation is substituted by *MaxSDev*. Note that the matched pattern is defined as the valid pattern of which the statistical mean has the minimum absolute difference with that of the latest duration sequence. As for the second type, it is identified when the standard deviation of the latest duration sequence is larger than that of the matched pattern but smaller than *MaxSDev*. In this case, the next value of the sequence will probably be a turning point since it is on the edge of two different patterns according to our pattern recognition process. Therefore, the mean of the next value is specified with the associated turning point of its matched pattern and the standard deviation is specified with *MaxSDev*. For the third type of sequence whose standard deviation is smaller than its matched pattern, the next value is predicted with the statistical features of the matched patterns as a refinement to that of the latest duration sequence. As presented in Table 5.5, we illustrate the specification of duration intervals with normal distribution, which is a kind of symmetric probability distribution. For example, given λ which is the $\alpha\%$ confidence percentile for normal distribution, the predicted $\alpha\%$ confidence interval is $(\mu - \lambda\sigma, \mu + \lambda\sigma)$, where μ and σ stand for the statistical sample mean and standard deviation, respectively. In our strategy, μ and σ are specified according to different types of duration sequences. However, if the duration samples of a pattern follow non-normal distribution models, such as uniform and exponential, changes can be made to the predicted intervals accordingly [92].

5.4   Evaluation

In this section, we demonstrate the results of large-scale comprehensive simulation experiments to verify the performance of our time-series-pattern-based interval forecasting strategy over the other representative strategies in the cloud workflow system SwinDeW-C. The simulation data and related materials can be found online[1].

5.4.1   Example Forecasting Process

In this section, an example is first presented to illustrate the whole forecasting process in detail. Afterwards, the results of a large-scale comparison experiment are demonstrated. Specifically, on the performance of time-series segmentation, the three generic time-series segmentation algorithms — Sliding Windows, Top-Down and Bottom-Up — are compared with our novel hybrid algorithm, $K-MaxSDev$. On the performance of interval forecasting, six representative time-series forecasting strategies widely used in traditional workflow systems, including LAST, MEAN, ES, MA, AR and NWS, are compared with our statistical time-series-pattern-based interval forecasting strategy based on the same samples.

---

[1] http://www.ict.swin.edu.au/personal/xliu/doc/IntervalForecasting.rar

Here, we illustrate an example forecasting process. To ensure the representativeness, a selection process is first conducted in workflow specifications to search for those activities which are both computation and data intensive and also with moderate mean durations according to the statistics of the system logs. Here, we randomly choose one of them to demonstrate the detailed forecasting process. Now, we demonstrate the simulation experiment with each step addressed in Section 5.3.4.

1. *Duration-series building*: The first step is to build the duration series. Here, we set the basic observation time unit as 15 minutes and the overall observation window as a typical working day of (8:00 a.m.−8:00 p.m.). As depicted in Figure 5.2A, with the period of a day, 15 duration series are built by random sampling without replacement in each observation unit. Here, null values are replaced by the unit sample means plus white noise [54], i.e. a random number with the mean of 0 and standard deviation of 1. Eventually, the representative duration series is built by the composition of the sample mean in each observation unit sequentially through the time. As depicted in Figure 5.2B, the representative

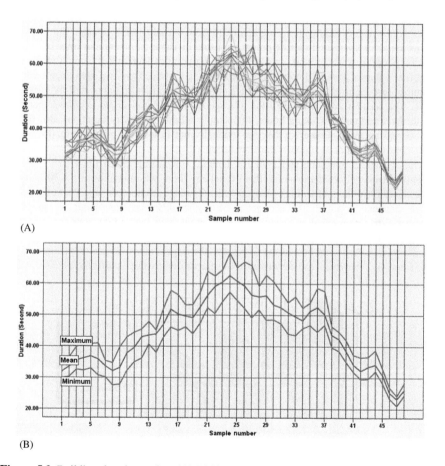

(A)

(B)

Figure 5.2 Building duration series: (A) 15 historical duration series; (B) the representative duration series.

duration series which is to be further analysed lies between the upper and the lower duration series which are composed of the maximum duration and minimum duration of each observation unit, respectively. In Figure 5.2, the vertical axis stands for the activity durations with the basic time unit of second.

2. Duration pattern recognition. In this step, we first conduct the $K-MaxSDev$ time-series segmentation algorithm to discover the potential pattern set. Here, we need to assign the value for two parameters: K and $MaxSDev$. Based on our empirical function, we choose the candidates of 2, 4, 8 and 12. With Formula (5.1) in Section 5.3.3, 5.3.4 is ranked the best. As for $MaxSDev$, based on Formula (5.2) in Section 5.3.3 with the overall sample mean μ as 44.11 and having the candidates of m as 15, 20, 25 and 30, they are specified as 2.21, 2.94, 3.68 and 4.41, respectively. We conduct $K-MaxSDev$ and compare with the three generic segmentation algorithms. With different $MaxSDev$, the number of segments for the four rounds of test is presented in Figure 5.3. Evidently, with 11, 8, 7 and 5 as the minimum number of segments in each round of testing, $K-MaxSDev$ achieves the best performance in terms of discovering the smallest potential pattern set.

   Moreover, with $MaxSDev$ as 2.21 and $Min\_pattern\_length$ as 3, which is the lowest bound, the result for segmentation and pattern validation is presented as an example in Table 5.6 where 8 valid patterns are identified from a total of 11 segments. The valid patterns and their associated turning points are listed in Table 5.7. Note that since our observation period is a whole working day, the turning point of Pattern 8 is actually defined as the first value of Pattern 1 to make it complete as a cycle. Here, we also trace back the number of concurrent activities according to the observation units covered by each pattern. The result shows that when the average number of concurrent activities increases with the schedule of working hours, the sample means of activity durations also follow an increasing trend. However, they are evidently not in a linear relationship. Therefore, this observation indeed supports our motivation.

3. Duration pattern matching and Duration interval forecasting. Since these two steps are highly correlated, we demonstrate them together. Here, we randomly select 30 duration sequences from the system logs where the lengths range from 4 to 6, and the last value of each sequence is chosen as the target to be predicted. In our experiment, we adopt the normal distribution model to specify the duration intervals with a high confidence of 95% [92]. As shown in Figure 5.4, for 25 cases, the target value lies within the predicted duration intervals. As for the rest of the five cases, the target values deviate only slightly from the intervals. Therefore, the performance of interval forecasting is effective.

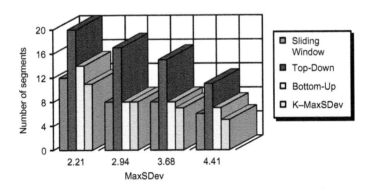

Figure 5.3 Comparison with three generic segmentation algorithms.

Table 5.6 Results for Segmentation and Pattern Validation

Segments	Segments Description			Covered Observation Time Units	Pattern Validation
	Mean	SDev	Length		
Segment 1	34.7	2.05	10	(8:00 a.m.−10:30 a.m.)	Valid
Segment 2	39.58	0	1	(10:30 a.m.−10:45 a.m.)	Invalid
Segment 3	44.47	0.47	3	(10:45 a.m.−11:30 a.m.)	Valid
Segment 4	50.10	2.00	6	(11:30 p.m.−1:00 p.m.)	Valid
Segment 5	59.81	2.10	6	(1:00 p.m.−2:30 p.m.)	Valid
Segment 6	55.43	1.45	4	(2:30 p.m.−3:30 p.m.)	Valid
Segment 7	50.75	1.51	7	(3:30 p.m.−5:15 p.m.)	Valid
Segment 8	43.00	0.94	2	(5:15 p.m.−5:45 p.m.)	Invalid
Segment 9	38.55	0	1	(5:45 p.m.−6:00 p.m.)	Invalid
Segment 10	33.01	1.45	5	(6:00 p.m.−7:15 p.m.)	Valid
Segment 11	24.88	1.49	3	(7:15 p.m.−8:00 p.m.)	Valid

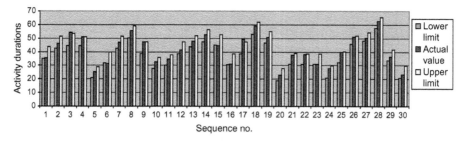

Table 5.7 Pattern Description and Associated Turning Points

Patterns	Patterns Description			Concurrent Activities
	Mean	SDev	Turning Points	
Pattern 1	34.7	2.05	39.58	(2, 4)
Pattern 2	44.47	0.47	46.98	(3, 6)
Pattern 3	50.10	2.00	56.33	(4, 8)
Pattern 4	59.81	2.10	56.35	(7, 11)
Pattern 5	55.43	1.45	52.42	(6, 10)
Pattern 6	50.75	1.51	43.00	(4, 9)
Pattern 7	33.01	1.45	25.22	(2, 5)
Pattern 8	24.88	1.49	31.99	(1, 3)

Figure 5.4 Predicted duration intervals.

5.4.2 Comparison Results

Here, we first demonstrate the comparison results on the performance of time-series segmentation. Similar to the example presented above, a total of 100 test cases of time series, each standing for an independent activity, are randomly selected and tested with a segmentation algorithm. As discussed in Section 5.3.3, given the same testing criterion, i.e. with the *MaxSDev*, the smaller the number of segments, the better the segmentation performance is.

As can be seen in Figure 5.5, in most cases our novel hybrid time-series segmentation algorithm $K-MaxSDev$ behaves the best and achieves the minimal number of segments which builds up the effective basis for time-series pattern recognition. Sliding Windows ranks in second place, but since it lacks the ability to look backwards, it tends to over segment when the system performance is stable (i.e. the number of segments is small) such as in the test cases of 11, 33, 48 and 53. Bottom-Up ranks in third place but since it lacks the ability to split, it tends to over segment when the system performance is dynamic such as in the test cases of 12, 20, 47 and 76. When the system performance is less dynamic (e.g. the number of segments is around 4−5 as depicted in Figure 5.5), its performance is close to that of Sliding Windows. Top-Down behaves the worst in most cases due to its tendency to over segment. Since the only action for Top-Down is splitting and since it stops the segmentation process as long as the testing criterion is met, Top-Down ignores the probability of merging small segments into large ones. Therefore, Top-Down usually has more segments than others.

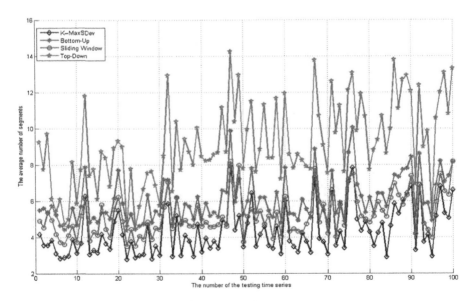

Figure 5.5 Performance on time-series segmentation.

Before we demonstrate the comparison results on the accuracy of interval forecasting, we briefly review the six representative forecasting strategies and introduce the setting of their parameters. Here, the actual value of the k_{th} point is denoted as Y_k, and the predicted value for the k_{th} point is denoted as P_k. The length of the latest duration sequence is randomly selected from 4 to 8.

1. LAST: LAST takes the last value of the time series as the predicted value for the next point. Therefore, Formula (5.3) for LAST is defined as follows:

$$P_k = Y_{k-1} \quad (k \geq 1) \tag{5.3}$$

   In the experiments, LAST takes the last point of the latest duration sequence as the predicted value.

2. MEAN: MEAN takes the mean value of all its previous points as the predicted value for the next point. Therefore, Formula (5.4) for LAST is defined as follows:

$$P_k = \frac{1}{k} \sum_{i=0}^{k-1} Y_i \quad (k \geq 1) \tag{5.4}$$

   In the experiments, MEAN takes the mean value of the entire time series to which the latest duration sequence belongs.

3. ES: ES makes the prediction for the next value based on both the actual value and the predicted value of its previous point. ES does not react directly to peaks while it reacts fast enough to significant changes of the mean values (e.g. the changes from one segment to another segment). The parameter α depends on the characteristics of the data set. The Formula (5.5) for ES is defined as follows:

$$P_k = Y_{k-1} + (1 - \alpha)P_{k-1} \quad (0 < \alpha < 1) \tag{5.5}$$

   In the experiments, ES applies to the latest duration sequence with α as 0.5 (a common choice given no prior knowledge).

4. MA: The generic MA predicts the next value based on the average value of the latest K points, denoted as MA(K). There are also many other modified versions of MA such as the Weighted MA and Exponential MA [35]. Formula (5.6) for the generic MA(K) is defined as follows:

$$P_{i+k} = \frac{1}{k} \sum_{j=i}^{i+k-1} Y_i \quad (i \geq 0, k \geq 1) \tag{5.6}$$

   In the experiments, MA applies to the latest duration sequence, and K is set randomly from 4 to 8, i.e. the average length of the duration sequences.

5. AR: AR multiplies previous data points with some parameters between 0 and 1 to predict the next value. These parameters can be deemed as weights assigned for each point where normally the closer the time, the larger the weight is. Formula (5.7) for the generic AR (K) is defined as follows:

$$P_{i+k} = \alpha_i Y_i + \alpha_{i+1} Y_{i+1} + \cdots + \alpha_{i+k-1} Y_{i+k-1} \quad \left(\sum_{j=i}^{i+k-1} \alpha_j = 1 \right) \tag{5.7}$$

In the experiments, the value of α_i is defined according to Formula (5.8):

$$\alpha_i = \begin{cases} 1 - \displaystyle\sum_{i=2}^{K} \alpha_i, & i = 1 \\[2ex] \dfrac{1}{Dis^2 \times 0.9}, & 2 \leq Dis \leq K \end{cases} \tag{5.8}$$

Here, the distance of the points, denoted as Dis, is defined based on the positions, i.e. for the last point in the latest duration sequence, its Dis is defined as 1, and for the second last, its Dis is defined as 2 and so forth. Obviously, as defined in Formula (5.8), the weight of each point decreases as its distance increases.

6. NWS: NWS conducts postcasters using different windows of previous data and records the 'winning' forecaster for each window size, i.e. the one with the minimal prediction errors on the last point afterwards, the predicted value will be the one predicted by the winning forecaster. The common forecasters included are Mean/Median, MA/Median, LAST and ES. Therefore, the formula for the NWS can be described using the following formula:

$$P_k = P_k | \{forecaster_i | Min(Err(P_{k-1}|forecaster_i))\} \quad (k \geq 1) \tag{5.9}$$

In the experiments, the forecasters included in NWS are all the other five forecasting strategies listed here. Therefore, based on the current performance, NWS dynamically selects the best forecasting strategies among LAST, MEAN, ES, MA and AR.

The comparison results on the accuracy of interval forecasting are presented in Figure 5.6. Here, accuracy means that the actual value is within the predicted interval.

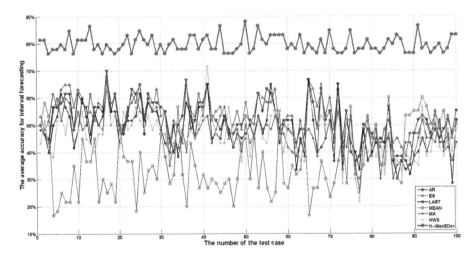

Figure 5.6 Accuracy of interval forecasting.

A total of 100 test cases, namely duration sequences, are randomly selected from those duration series with the mean durations around 20–40 minutes and applied with each forecasting strategy. Since despite our $K-MaxSDev$, all the other forecasting algorithms are all dedicated to point forecasting, in the experiments their upper bounds and lower bounds are defined as the predicted value plus 10% of itself and the predicted value minus 10% of itself, respectively. Therefore, an interval with the length of 20% of the predicted value is created.

As can be seen in Figure 5.6, our pattern-based forecasting strategy (denoted as $K-MaxSDev$) gains a large improvement on the average accuracy of interval forecasting over the other representative forecasting strategies. The average accuracy of our $K-MaxSDev$ is 80% while that of the other strategies is generally around 40–50%. Among the other six strategies, AR behaves the best while the others have similar performance — except MEAN, which behaves poorly compared with the others. However, such results actually demonstrate the highly dynamic performance of the underlying services in cloud workflow systems.

To conclude, in comparison to other representative forecasting strategies in traditional workflow systems, our forecasting strategy can effectively address the problems of limited sample size and frequent turning points and hence achieve higher accuracy.

6 Temporal Constraint Setting

As one of the most important workflow QoS dimensions and the focus in this book, the temporal constraint is the foundation of the entire temporal framework. Temporal constraint setting deals with temporal QoS specifications at workflow build time. As mentioned earlier, high temporal QoS cannot be achieved without proper setting of high-quality temporal constraints.

This chapter presents a probabilistic strategy for setting temporal constraints. Section 6.1 introduces the specifically related work and problem analysis. Section 6.2 presents probability-based temporal consistency model. Section 6.3 illustrates the detailed process for setting temporal constraints. Section 6.4 describes a case study to demonstrate the effectiveness of the setting strategy.

This chapter is mainly based on our work presented in Refs [61,62].

6.1   Related Work and Problem Analysis

6.1.1   Related Work

In this section, we review related work on temporal constraints in workflow systems. The work in Ref. [103] presents the taxonomy of grid workflow QoS constraints which include five dimensions, namely time, cost, fidelity, reliability and security. Some papers have presented the overview analysis of scientific workflow QoS [50,55,70]. The work in Ref. [20] presents the taxonomy of grid workflow verification which includes the verification of temporal constraints. In a distributed environment such as a distributed soft real-time system, a task (workflow process) is usually divided into several subtasks (workflow activities) to be executed in a specific order at different sites. Therefore, the issue of automatically translating the overall deadline into deadlines for the individual subtasks is investigated in Refs [17,52]. Generally speaking, there are two basic ways to assign QoS constraints: one is activity-level assignment and the other is workflow-level assignment. Since the whole workflow process is composed of individual activities, an overall workflow-level constraint can be obtained from the composition of activity-level constraints. On the contrary, activity-level constraints can also be assigned by the decomposition of workflow-level constraints [103]. However, different QoS constraints have their own characteristics which require in-depth research to handle different scenarios.

Temporal QoS Management in Scientific Cloud Workflow Systems. DOI: 10.1016/B978-0-12-397010-7.00006-9

The primary information required for temporal constraint setting includes the workflow process models, statistics of activity durations and the temporal consistency model. Scientific workflows require the explicit representation of temporal information, i.e. activity durations and temporal constraints, to facilitate temporal verification. One of the classical modelling methods is the Stochastic Petri Nets [3,9] which incorporates time and probability attributes into workflow processes that can be employed to facilitate scientific workflow modelling. Activity duration, as one of the basic elements to measure system performance, is of significant value to workflow scheduling, performance analysis and temporal verification [19,21,91,105]. Most work obtains activity durations from workflow system logs and describes them by a discrete or continuous probability distribution through statistical analysis [3,61,92]. As for temporal consistency, traditionally, there are only binary states of consistency or inconsistency. However, as stated in Ref. [18], it is argued that the conventional consistency condition is too restrictive and covers several different states which should be handled differently for the purpose of cost-effectiveness. Therefore, it divides conventional inconsistency into weak consistency, weak inconsistency and strong inconsistency and treats them accordingly. However, a multiple-state-based temporal consistency model cannot support quantitative measurement of temporal consistency states and lacks the ability to support statistical analysis for constraint management. Therefore, in our work [61], a probability-based build-time temporal consistency model is presented to facilitate the setting of temporal constraints.

Temporal constraints are not well emphasised in traditional workflow systems. However, some business workflow systems accommodate temporal information for the purpose of performance analysis. For example, Staffware provides the audit trail tool to monitor the execution of individual instances [2] and SAP business workflow system employs the workload analysis [56]. As for the support of temporal constraints in scientific workflow systems, an overview of the support of temporal constraints in representative scientific workflow systems is conducted by us and based on some of the work reported in Refs [20,103]. Since workflow modelling is highly related to the specification of temporal constraints, the overview also deals with two aspects of the modelling language and the modelling tool (language based, graph based or both) in addition to the three aspects of whether they support the specification of temporal constraints (the specification of temporal constraints in workflow models), the management of temporal constraints (i.e. the setting and updating of temporal constraints) or the temporal verification (the verification of temporal constraints).

As shown in Table 6.1, among the 10 representative scientific workflow projects (ASKALON [78], CROWN workflow component [79], DAGMan [31], GridBus [80], JOpera [81], Kepler [82], SwinDeW-G [100], Taverna [84], Triana [83] and UNICORE [85]), most projects use XML-like modelling language and support language-based or graph-based modelling tools. Therefore, in the modelling stage, a temporal constraint can be specified either inexplicitly as an element in the XML document or explicitly as a graphic component in the workflow template. As for the representation of temporal constraints, the management of temporal constraints

Table 6.1 Overview on the Support of Temporal QoS Constraints

Scientific Workflow Systems	Modelling Language	Modelling Tool	Temporal Constraint Specification	Temporal Constraint Management	Temporal Constraint Verification
ASKALON	AGWL	Language based Graph based	Supported	N/A	N/A
CROWN	GPEL	Language based	N/A	N/A	N/A
DAGMan	DAG Scripts	Language based	Supported	N/A	N/A
GridBus	xWFL	Language based Graph based	Supported	N/A	N/A
JOpera	JVCL	Language based Graph based	Supported	N/A	N/A
Kepler	SDF	Graph based	Supported	N/A	N/A
SwinDeW-G	XPDL/ BPEL	Graph based	Supported	Supported	Supported
Taverna	SCUFL	Language based Graph based	Supported	N/A	N/A
Triana	WSFL	Language based Graph based	N/A	N/A	N/A
UNICORE	BPEL	Language based Graph based	N/A	N/A	N/A

and the support of temporal verification with which we are most concerned, only some of the projects (such as ASKALON, DAGMan, GridBus, JOpera, Kepler, Taverna and SwinDeW-G), clearly state in their published literatures that temporal constraints are supported in their system QoS control or performance analysis. Yet, to our best knowledge, only SwinDeW-G has set up a series of strategies such as the probabilistic strategy for temporal constraint management [61] and the efficient checkpoint selection strategy to support dynamic temporal verification [21]. In summary, even though temporal QoS has been recognised as an important aspect of scientific workflow systems, the work in this area, e.g. the specification of temporal constraints and the support of temporal verification, is still in its infancy [20].

6.1.2 Problem Analysis

Setting temporal constraints is not a trivial task. Many factors such as workflow structures, system performance and user requirements should be taken into consideration. Here, we present the basic requirements for temporal constraint setting by analysing two criteria for high-quality temporal constraints.

1. Temporal constraints should be well balanced between user requirements and system performance. Users often suggest coarse-grained temporal constraints based on their own interest although they have limited knowledge about the actual performance of workflow systems. For example, it is not rational to set a 60-minute temporal constraint to a

segment which normally needs two hours to finish. Therefore, user-specified constraints often cause frequent temporal violations. To address this problem, a negotiation process between the user and the service provider who is well aware of the system performance is desirable to derive balanced coarse-grained temporal constraints with which both sides are satisfied.

2. Temporal constraints should facilitate both overall coarse-grained control and local fine-grained control. As analysed above, this criterion actually means that temporal constraint setting should support both coarse-grained temporal constraints and fine-grained temporal constraints. Specifically, the task of setting build-time temporal constraints includes setting both coarse-grained temporal constraints (a global deadline for the entire workflow instance and several milestones for local workflow segments) and fine-grained temporal constraints (temporal constraints for individual workflow activities). However, although the overall workflow process is composed of individual workflow activities, coarse-grained temporal constraints and fine-grained temporal constraints are not in a simple relationship of linear culmination and decomposition. Meanwhile, it is impractical to set or update fine-grained temporal constraints manually for a large number of activities in scientific workflows. Since coarse-grained temporal constraints can be obtained through the negotiation process, the problem in setting fine-grained temporal constraints is how to automatically derive them based on the coarse-grained temporal constraints.

To conclude, the basic requirements for temporal constraint setting in scientific cloud workflow systems can be summed up as (a) effective negotiation for setting coarse-grained temporal constraints and (b) automatically deriving fine-grained temporal constraints.

6.2   Probability-based Temporal Consistency Model

In this section, we present a novel probability-based temporal consistency model which utilises the weighted joint distribution of workflow activity durations to facilitate temporal constraint setting in scientific workflow systems.

6.2.1   Weighted Joint Normal Distribution for Workflow Activity Durations

To define the weighted joint distribution of workflow activity durations, we first present two assumptions about the probability distribution of activity durations.

Assumption 1. The distribution of activity durations can be obtained from workflow system logs through statistical analysis [59]. Without losing generality, we assume that all the activity durations follow the normal distribution model, which can be denoted as $N(\mu,\sigma^2)$ where μ is the expected value, σ^2 is the variance and σ is the standard deviation [92].

Assumption 2. The activity durations are independent from each other.
For the convenience of analysis, Assumption 1 chooses normal distribution to model the activity durations without losing generality. If most of the activity

durations follow non-normal distribution, e.g. uniform, exponential, lognormal or beta distribution [54], the idea of our strategy can still be applied in a similar way given different joint distribution models. However, we will leave the detailed investigation of different distribution models as our future work. Furthermore, as it is commonly applied in the area of system simulation and performance analysis, Assumption 2 requires that the activity durations be independent from each other to facilitate the analysis of joint normal distribution. For those which do not follow the above assumptions, they can be treated by normal transformation and correlation analysis [92], or moreover, they can be ignored first when calculating joint distribution and then added up afterwards.

Furthermore, we present an important formula, Formula (6.1), of joint normal distribution.

If there are n independent variables of $X_i \sim N(\mu_i, \sigma_i^2)$ and n real numbers θ_i, where n is a natural number, then the joint distribution of these variables can be obtained with the following formula [92]:

$$Z = \theta_1 X_1 + \theta_2 X_2 + \cdots + \theta_n X_n = \sum_{i=1}^{n} \theta_i X_i \sim N\left(\sum_{i=1}^{n} \theta_i \mu_i, \sum_{i=1}^{n} \theta_i^2 \sigma_i^2\right) \tag{6.1}$$

Based on this formula, we define the weighted joint distribution of workflow activity durations as follows.

Definition 6.1. (Weighted joint distribution). For a scientific workflow process SW which consists of n activities, we denote the activity duration distribution of activity a_i as $N(\mu_i, \sigma_i^2)$ with $1 \leq i \leq n$. Then the weighted joint distribution is defined as $N(\mu_{sw}, \sigma_{sw}^2) = N\left(\sum_{i=1}^{n} w_i \mu_i, \sum_{i=1}^{n} w_i^2 \sigma_i^2\right)$, where w_i stands for the weight of activity a_i that denotes the choice probability or iteration times associated with the workflow path to which a_i belongs.

The weight of each activity with different workflow structures is illustrated through the calculation of weighted joint distribution for basic Stochastic Petri-Nets-based building blocks, i.e. sequence, iteration, parallelism and choice. These four building blocks consist of basic control flow patterns and are widely used in workflow modelling and structure analysis [2,3]. Most workflow process models can be easily built by their compositions and similarly for the weighted joint distribution of most workflow processes. Here, Stochastic Petri-Nets-based modelling [3] is employed to incorporate time and probability attributes with additional graphic notations, e.g. ⬣ stands for the probability of the path and ⬚ stands for the normal duration distribution of the associated activity. For simplicity, we illustrate with two paths for the iteration, parallelism and choice building blocks, except the sequence building block which has only one path by nature. However, the results can be effectively extended to more than two paths in a similar way.

1. *Sequence building block*: As depicted in Figure 6.1, the sequence building block is composed by adjacent activities from a_i to a_j in a sequential relationship which means the

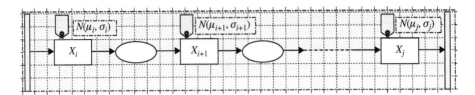

Figure 6.1 Sequence building block.

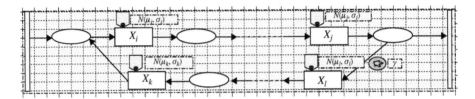

Figure 6.2 Iteration building block.

successor activity will not be executed until its predecessor activity is finished. The structure weight for each activity in the sequence building block is 1 since each one needs to be executed only once. Therefore, according to Formula (6.1), the weighted joint distribution is $Z = \sum_{k=i}^{j} X_k \sim N\left(\left(\sum_{k=i}^{j} \mu_k\right), \left(\sum_{k=i}^{j} \sigma_k^2\right)\right)$.

2. *Iteration building block*: As depicted in Figure 6.2, the iteration building block contains two paths which are executed iteratively until certain end conditions are satisfied. Without the context of run-time workflow execution, it is difficult, if not impossible, to obtain the number of iteration times at workflow build time. Therefore, in practice, the number of iteration times is usually estimated with the mean iteration times or with some probability distribution models such as normal, uniform or exponential distribution. In this chapter, we use the mean iteration times to calculate the weighted joint distribution in the iteration building block. The major advantage for this simplification is to avoid the complex joint distribution (if exists) of activity durations (normal distribution) and the number of iteration times (may be normal or other non-normal distribution) in order to facilitate the setting of temporal constraints at build time in an efficient fashion. Here, to be consistent with the Stochastic Petri Nets, we assume that the probability of meeting the end conditions for a single iteration is ρ (i.e. the mean iteration time is $1/\rho$) as denoted by the probability notation. Therefore, the lower path is expected to be executed for $1/\rho$ times and hence the upper path is executed for $(1/\rho) + 1$ times. Accordingly, the structure weight for each activity in the iteration building block is the expected execution times the path it belongs to. The weighted joint distribution here is $Z = ((1/\rho) + 1)\left(\sum_{p=i}^{j} X_p\right) + (1/\rho)\left(\sum_{q=k}^{l} X_q\right) \sim$

$N\left(((1/\rho) + 1)\left(\sum_{p=i}^{j} \mu_p\right) + (1/\rho)\left(\sum_{q=k}^{l} \mu_q\right), ((1/\rho) + 1)^2 \left(\sum_{p=i}^{j} \sigma_p^2\right) + (1/\rho)^2 \left(\sum_{q=k}^{l} \sigma_q^2\right)\right)$.

3. *Parallelism building block*: As depicted in Figure 6.3, the parallelism building block contains two paths which are executed in parallel. Since the activity durations are modelled by normal distributed variables, the overall duration time of the parallelism building block is equal to the distribution of the maximum duration of the two parallel paths. However, to calculate the exact distribution of the maximum of two random variables is

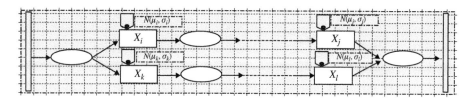

Figure 6.3 Parallelism building block.

a complex issue [72] which requires fundamental knowledge on statistics and non-trivial computation cost. Therefore, in practice, approximation is often applied instead of using the exact distribution. Since the overall completion time of the parallelism building block is dominated by the path with the longer duration [3], in this book, we define the joint distribution of the parallelism building block as the joint distribution of the path with a lager expected duration, i.e. if $\sum_{p=i}^{j} \mu_p \geq \sum_{q=k}^{l} \mu_q$ then $Z = \sum_{p=i}^{j} \mu_p$, otherwise $Z = \sum_{q=k}^{l} \mu_q$. Accordingly, the structure weight for each activity on the path with longer duration is 1, while on the other path it is 0. Therefore, the weighted joint distribution of this block is

$$
Z = \begin{cases} \sum_{p=i}^{j} X_p \sim N\left(\sum_{p=i}^{j} \mu_p, \sum_{p=i}^{j} \sigma_p^2\right), & \text{if } \sum_{p=i}^{j} \mu_p \geq \sum_{q=k}^{l} \mu_q \\ \sum_{q=k}^{l} X_q \sim N\left(\sum_{q=k}^{l} \mu_q, \sum_{q=k}^{l} \sigma_q^2\right), & \text{otherwise} \end{cases}.
$$

4. *Choice building block*: As depicted in Figure 6.4, the choice building block contains two paths in an exclusive relationship which means that only one path will be executed at run-time. The probability notation denotes that the probability for the choice of the upper path is β, and hence the choice probability for the lower path is $1 - \beta$. In the real world, β may also follow some probability distribution. However, similar to the iteration building block, in order to avoid the complex joint distribution, β is estimated by the mean probability for selecting a specific path, i.e. the number of times that the path has been selected divided by the total number of workflow instances. Accordingly, the structure weight for each activity in the choice building block is the probability of the path it belongs to. The weighted joint distribution is $Z = \beta\left(\sum_{p=i}^{j} X_p\right) + (1 - \beta)\left(\sum_{q=k}^{l} X_q\right) \sim N\left(\beta\left(\sum_{p=i}^{j} \mu_p\right) + (1 - \beta)\left(\sum_{q=k}^{l} \mu_q\right), \beta^2\left(\sum_{p=i}^{j} \sigma_p^2\right) + (1 - \beta)^2\left(\sum_{q=k}^{l} \sigma_p^2\right)\right)$.

Note that the purpose of presenting the weighted joint normal distribution of the four basic building blocks is twofold. The first is to illustrate the definition of structure weight for workflow activity durations. The second is to facilitate the efficient calculation of weighted joint normal distribution of scientific workflows or workflow segments at build time by the composition of the four basic building blocks. Furthermore, following the common practice in the workflow area [3,91], approximation has been made to avoid calculating complex joint distribution. Since it is not the focus of this chapter, the discussion on the exact distribution of these complex joint distribution models can be found in Refs [72,92].

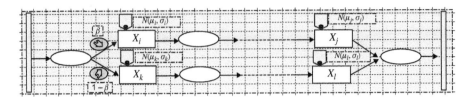

Figure 6.4 Choice building block.

6.2.2 Probability-based Temporal Consistency Model

The weighted joint distribution enables us to analyse the completion time of the entire workflow from an overall perspective. Here, we need to define some notations. For a workflow activity a_i, its maximum duration, mean duration and minimum duration are defined as $D(a_i)$, $M(a_i)$ and $d(a_i)$, respectively. For a scientific workflow SW which consists of n activities, its build-time upper bound temporal constraint is denoted as $U(SW)$. In addition, we employ the '3σ' rule which has been widely used in statistical data analysis to specify the possible intervals of activity durations [54]. The '3σ' rule depicts that for any sample coming from normal distribution model, it has a probability of 99.73% to fall into the range of $[\mu - 3\sigma, \mu + 3\sigma]$ which is a symmetric interval of three standard deviations around the mean where μ and σ are the sample mean and sample standard deviation, respectively. The statistical information can be obtained through scientific workflow system logs through statistical analysis [59]. Therefore, in this book, we define the maximum duration, the mean duration and the minimum duration as $D(a_i) = \mu_i + 3\sigma_i$, $M(a_i) = \mu_i$ and $d(a_i) = \mu_i - 3\sigma_i$, respectively. Accordingly, samples from the scientific workflow system logs which are above $D(a_i)$ or below $d(a_i)$ are hence discarded as outliers. The actual run-time duration at a_i is denoted as $R(a_i)$. Now, we present the definition of probability-based temporal consistency which is based on the weighted joint distribution of activity durations. Note that, since our temporal framework includes both build-time components and run-time components to support the lifecycle of scientific workflow systems, our probability-based temporal consistency model also includes both definitions for build-time temporal consistency and run-time temporal consistency.

Definition 6.2. (Probability-based temporal consistency model). At build-time stage, $U(SW)$ is said to be:

1. Absolute Consistency (AC), if $\sum_{i=1}^{n} w_i(\mu_i + 3\sigma_i) < U(SW)$;
2. Absolute Inconsistency (AI), if $\sum_{i=1}^{n} w_i(\mu_i - 3\sigma_i) > U(SW)$;
3. $\alpha\%$ Consistency ($\alpha\%$ C), if $\sum_{i=1}^{n} w_i(\mu_i + \lambda\sigma_i) = U(SW)$.

At run-time stage, at a workflow activity a_p ($1 < p < n$), $U(SW)$ is said to be:

1. AC, if $\sum_{i=1}^{p} R(a_i) + \sum_{j=p+1}^{n} w_i(\mu_i + 3\sigma_i) < U(SW)$;
2. AI, if $\sum_{i=1}^{p} R(a_i) + \sum_{j=p+1}^{n} w_i(\mu_i - 3\sigma_i) > U(SW)$;
3. $\alpha\%$ C, if $\sum_{i=1}^{p} R(a_i) + \sum_{j=p+1}^{n} w_i(\mu_i + \lambda\sigma_i) = U(SW)$.

Here w_i stands for the weight of activity a_i, λ $(-3 \leq \lambda \leq 3)$ is defined as the $\alpha\%$ confidence percentile with the cumulative normal distribution function of $F(\mu_i + \lambda\sigma_i) = \frac{1}{\sigma\sqrt{2\pi}} \int_{-\infty}^{\mu_i + \lambda\sigma_i} \ell^{-(x-\mu_i)^2/2\sigma_i^2} \cdot dx = \alpha\%$ $(0 < \alpha < 100)$.

Note that the build-time model will mainly be used in Component I, and its run-time counterpart will mainly be used in Components II and III of this book. Meanwhile, as explained in Ref. [67], without losing generality, the weights of activities may be omitted for the ease of discussion in the subsequent chapters for run-time components.

As depicted in Figure 6.5, different from conventional multiple temporal consistency model where only four discrete coarse-grained temporal consistency states are defined [18,22], in our temporal consistency model, every probability temporal consistency state is represented by a unique probability value and together they compose a Gaussian curve the same as the cumulative normal distribution [54]. Therefore, they can effectively support the requirements of both coarse-grained control and fine-grained control in scientific workflow systems as discussed in Section 6.1.2. The probability consistency states outside the confidence percentile interval of $[-3, +3]$ are with continuous values infinitely approaching 0% or 100%, respectively. However, since there are scarce chances (i.e. $1 - 99.73\% = 0.17\%$) that the probability temporal consistency state will fall outside this interval, we name them AC and AI in order to distinguish them from others.

The purpose of probability-based temporal consistency is to facilitate the setting of temporal constraints in scientific workflow systems. The advantage of the novel temporal consistency model mainly includes three aspects. First, service users normally cannot distinguish between qualitative expressions such as weak consistency and weak inconsistency due to the lack of background knowledge and thus deteriorate the negotiation process for setting coarse-grained temporal constraints at build time. In contrast, a quantitative temporal consistency state of 90% or 80% makes much more sense. Second, it is better to model activity duration as random variables instead of static time attributes in system environments with highly dynamic performance to facilitate statistical analysis. Third, to facilitate the setting of fine-

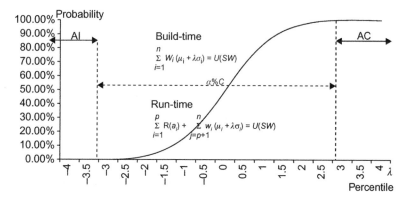

Figure 6.5 Probability-based temporal consistency model.

grained temporal constraints at build time, a continuous states-based temporal consistency model in which any fine-grained temporal consistency state is represented by a unique probability value is required rather than discrete multiple states-based temporal consistency model in which temporal consistency states are represented by coarse-grained qualitative expressions.

6.3   Setting Temporal Constraints

In this section, we present our negotiation-based probabilistic strategy for setting temporal constraints at build time. The strategy aims to effectively produce a set of coarse-grained and fine-grained temporal constraints which are well balanced between user requirements and system performance.

As depicted in Table 6.2, the strategy requires the input of process model and system logs. It consists of three steps: calculating weighted joint distribution, setting coarse-grained temporal constraints and setting fine-grained temporal constraints. We illustrate them accordingly in the following sub-sections.

6.3.1   Calculating Weighted Joint Distribution

The first step is to calculate weighted joint distribution. The statistic information, i.e. activity duration distribution and activity weight, can be obtained from system logs by statistical analysis [3,59]. Afterwards, given the input process model for the scientific workflow, the weighted joint distribution of activity durations for the

Table 6.2 Probabilistic Setting Strategy

Probabilistic Strategy for Setting Temporal Constraints	
Overview	Input: process model and system logs for scientific workflow
	Method: probabilistic setting strategy
	Output: coarse-grained upper bound constraints and fine-grained upper bound constraints
Step 1: Calculating weighted joint distribution	Obtain the statistic information (activity duration distribution and activity weight) from workflow system logs;
	Calculate the weighted joint distribution of the workflow by the composition of basic building blocks
Step 2: Setting coarse-grained constraints	Set coarse-grained temporal constraints through either the time-oriented or probability-oriented negotiation process based on weighted joint distribution and the probability-based temporal consistency
Step 3: Setting fine-grained constraints	Set fine-grained temporal constraints based on the same probability consistency as the coarse-grained temporal constraints obtained in Step 2

entire scientific workflow and workflow segments can be efficiently obtained from the composition of the four basic building blocks as illustrated in Section 6.2.1.

6.3.2   Setting Coarse-grained Temporal Constraints

The second step is to set coarse-grained upper bound temporal constraints at build time. Based on the four basic building blocks, the weighted joint distribution of an entire workflow or workflow segment can be obtained efficiently to facilitate the negotiation process for setting coarse-grained temporal constraints. Here, we denote the obtained weighted joint distribution of the target scientific workflow (or work-flow segment) SW as $N(\mu_{sw}, \sigma_{sw}^2)$ where $\mu_{sw} = \sum_{i=1}^{n} w_i \mu_i$ and $\sigma_{sw} = \sqrt{\sum_{i=1}^{n} w_i^2 \sigma_i^2}$. Meanwhile, we assume that the minimum threshold for the probability consistency is $\beta\%$, which implies the user's acceptable bottom-line probability, namely the confidence for timely completion of the workflow instance; and the maximum threshold for the upper bound constraint is $\max(SW)$, which denotes the user's acceptable latest completion time. The actual negotiation process can be conducted in two alternative ways: time oriented and probability oriented.

The time-oriented negotiation process starts with the user's initial suggestion of an upper bound temporal constraint of $U(SW)$ and the evaluation of the corresponding temporal consistency state by the service provider. If $U(SW) = \mu_{sw} + \sigma_{sw}$ with λ as the $\alpha\%$ percentile, and $\alpha\%$ is below the threshold of $\beta\%$, then the upper bound temporal constraint needs to be adjusted, otherwise the negotiation process terminates. The subsequent process is the iteration in which the user presents a new upper bound temporal constraint which is less constrained than the previous one and the service provider re-evaluates the consistency state until it reaches or is above the minimum probability threshold.

In contrast, the probability-oriented negotiation process begins with the user's initial suggestion of a probability value of $\alpha\%$. The service provider evaluates the execution time $R(SW)$ of the entire workflow process SW by the sum of all activity durations as $\sum_{i=1}^{n} w_i(\mu_i + \lambda \sigma_i)$, where λ is the $\alpha\%$ percentile. If $R(SW)$ is above the maximum upper bound constraint of $\max(SW)$ for the user, the probability value needs to be adjusted, otherwise the negotiation process terminates. The following process is the iteration in which the user presents a new probability value which is lower than the previous one and the service provider re-evaluates the workflow duration until it reaches or is lower than the upper bound constraint.

As depicted in Figure 6.6, with the probability-based temporal consistency, the time-oriented negotiation process is normally where increasing upper bound constraints are presented and evaluated with their temporal probability consistency states until the probability is above the user's bottom-line confidence; the probability-oriented negotiation process is normally where decreasing temporal probability consistency states are presented and estimated with their upper bound constraints until the constraint is below the user's acceptable latest completion time. In practice, the user and service provider can choose either of the two negotiation processes or even interchange dynamically if they want. However, on one hand, users who have some background knowledge about the execution time of the entire workflow or some of the

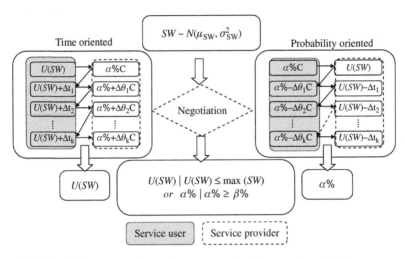

Figure 6.6 Negotiation process for setting coarse-grained temporal constraints.

workflow segments may prefer to choose time-oriented negotiation process since it is relatively easier for them to estimate and adjust the coarse-grained constraints. On the other hand, for users who have no sufficient background knowledge, a probability-oriented negotiation process is a better choice since they can make the decision by comparing the probability values of temporal consistency states with their personal bottom-line confidence values.

6.3.3 Setting Fine-grained Temporal Constraints

The third step is to set fine-grained temporal constraints. In fact, this process is straightforward with the probability-based temporal consistency model. Since our temporal consistency actually defines that if all the activities are executed with the duration of $\alpha\%$ probability and their total weighted duration equals their upper bound constraint, we say that the workflow process is $\alpha\%$ C at build time. For example, if the obtained probability consistency is 90% with the confidence percentile λ of 1.28 (the percentile value can be obtained from any normal distribution table or most statistical programme [92]), it means that all activities are expected for the duration of 90% probability. However, to ensure that the coarse-grained and fine-grained temporal constraints are consistent with the overall workflow execution time, the sum of weighted fine-grained temporal constraints should be approximate to their coarse-grained temporal constraint. Otherwise, even if the duration of every workflow activity satisfies its fine-grained temporal constraint, there is still a good chance that the overall coarse-grained temporal constraints will be violated, i.e. the workflow cannot complete on time. Therefore, based on the same percentile value, the fine-grained temporal constraint for each activity is defined with Formula (6.2) to make them consistent with their overall coarse-grained temporal constraint.

For a scientific workflow or workflow segment SW which has a coarse-grained temporal constraint of $U(SW)$ with $\alpha\%$ C of λ percentile, if SW consists of n workflow activities with $a_i \sim N(\mu_i, \sigma_i^2)$, the fine-grained upper bound temporal constraint for activity a_i is $U(a_i)$ and can be obtained with the following formula:

$$u(a_i) = \mu_i + \lambda\sigma_i \times \left(1 - \left(\sum_{i=1}^{n} w_i\sigma_i - \sqrt{\sum_{i=1}^{n} w_i^2\sigma_i^2}\right)\Big/ \sum_{i=1}^{n} \sigma_i\right) \tag{6.2}$$

Here, μ_i and σ_i are obtained directly from the mean value and standard deviation of activity a_i, and λ denotes the same probability as the coarse-grained temporal constraint. Based on Formula (6.2), we can claim that with our setting strategy, the sum of weighted fine-grained temporal constraints is approximately the same as their overall coarse-grained temporal constraint. Here, we present a theoretical proof to verify our claim.

Proof. Assume that the distribution model for the duration of activity a_i is $N(\mu_i, \sigma_i^2)$; hence, with Formula (6.1), the coarse-grained constraint is set to be of $u(SW) = \mu_{sw} + \lambda\sigma_{sw}$ where $\mu_{sw} = \sum_{i=1}^{n} w_i\mu_i$ and $\sigma_{sw} = \sqrt{\sum_{i=1}^{n} w_i^2\sigma_i^2}$. As defined in Formula (6.2), the sum of weighted fine-grained constraints is $\sum_{i=1}^{n} w_i u(a_i) = \sum_{i=1}^{n} w_i\left(\mu_i + \lambda\sigma_i \times \left(1 - \left(\sum_{i=1}^{n} w_i\sigma_i - \sqrt{\sum_{i=1}^{n} w_i^2\sigma_i^2}\right)\big/\sum_{i=1}^{n} \sigma_i\right)\right)$. Evidently, since w_i and σ_i are all positive values, $\sum_{i=1}^{n} w_i\sigma_i \geq \sqrt{\sum_{i=1}^{n} w_i^2\sigma_i^2}$ holds and $\sum_{i=1}^{n} \sigma_i$ is normally big for a large size scientific workflow SW, hence the right-hand side of the equation can be extended and what we get is $\sum_{i=1}^{n} w_i (\mu_i + \lambda\sigma_i \times (1 - A))$ where A equals $\left(\sum_{i=1}^{n} w_i\sigma_i - \sqrt{\sum_{i=1}^{n} w_i^2\sigma_i^2}\right)/\sum_{i=1}^{n} \sigma_i$. Therefore, it can be expressed as $\sum_{i=1}^{n} w_i u(a_i) = \sum_{i=1}^{n} w_i\mu_i + \lambda\sum_{i=1}^{n} w_i\sigma_i - \Delta t_1$ (Equation I) where $\Delta t_1 = \sum_{i=1}^{n} w_i A$. Meanwhile, since $\sum_{i=1}^{n} w_i\sigma_i \geq \sqrt{\sum_{i=1}^{n} w_i^2\sigma_i^2}$, thus $\sum_{i=1}^{n} w_i\mu_i + \lambda\sqrt{\sum_{i=1}^{n} w_i^2\sigma_i^2} \leq \sum_{i=1}^{n} w_i\mu_i + \lambda\sum_{i=1}^{n} w_i\sigma_i$. Therefore, it can be expressed as $u(WS) = \sum_{i=1}^{n} w_i\mu_i + \lambda\sqrt{\sum_{i=1}^{n} w_i^2\sigma_i^2} = \sum_{i=1}^{n} w_i\mu_i + \lambda\sum_{i=1}^{n} w_i\sigma_i - \Delta t_2$ (Equation II) where Δt_2 equals $\lambda(\sum_{i=1}^{n} w_i\sigma_i - \sqrt{\sum_{i=1}^{n} w_i^2\sigma_i^2})$. Furthermore, if we denote $(\sum_{i=1}^{n} w_i\sigma_i - \sqrt{\sum_{i=1}^{n} w_i^2\sigma_i^2})$ as B then we can have $\Delta t_1 = (\sum_{i=1}^{n} w_i/\sum_{i=1}^{n} \sigma_i)B$ and $\Delta t_2 = \lambda B$. Since in real-world scientific workflows, $(\sum_{i=1}^{n} w_i/\sum_{i=1}^{n} \sigma_i)$ is smaller than 1 due to $\sum_{i=1}^{n} \sigma_i$ being normally much bigger than $\sum_{i=1}^{n} w_i$, meanwhile, λ is a positive value smaller than 1 (1 means a probability consistency of 84.13% which is acceptable for most users) [92], Δt_1 and Δt_2 are all relatively small positive values compared with the major component of Equation I and Equation II above. Evidently, we can deduce that $\sum_{i=1}^{n} w_i u(a_i) = \sum_{i=1}^{n} w_i\mu_i + \lambda\sum_{i=1}^{n} w_i\sigma_i - \Delta t_1 \approx \sum_{i=1}^{n} w_i\mu_i + \lambda\sum_{i=1}^{n} w_i\sigma_i - \Delta t_2 = U(WS)$. Therefore, the sum of weighted fine-grained temporal constraints is approximately the same as the coarse-grained temporal constraint and thus our claim holds.

6.4   Case Study

In this section, we evaluate the effectiveness of our probabilistic strategy for setting temporal constraints by illustrating a case study on a data collection workflow segment in a weather forecast scientific workflow. The process model is the same as depicted in Figure 6.7. The entire weather forecast workflow contains hundreds of data-intensive and computation-intensive activities. Major data-intensive activities include the collection of meteorological information, e.g. surface data, atmospheric humidity, temperature, cloud area and wind speed from satellites, radars and ground observatories at distributed geographic locations. These data files are transferred via various kinds of networks. Computation-intensive activities mainly consist of solving complex meteorological equations, e.g. meteorological dynamics equations, thermodynamic equations, pressure equations, turbulent kinetic energy equations and so forth, which require high-performance computing resources. For the purposes of our case study, there is no point in presenting the whole forecasting process in detail. Here, we focus only on one of its segments for radar data collection. As depicted in Figure 6.7, this workflow segment contains 12 activities which are modelled by Stochastic Petri Nets with additional graphic notations as illustrated in Section 6.3.1. For simplicity, we denote these activities as X_1 to X_{12}. The workflow process structures are composed with four Stochastic Petri-Nets-based building blocks, i.e. a choice block for data collection from two radars at different locations (activities X_1-X_4), a compound block of parallelism and iteration for data updating and pre-processing (activities X_6-X_{10}) and two sequence blocks for data transferring (activities X_5 X_{11} X_{12}).

Here, we first illustrate our probabilistic strategy for setting build-time temporal constraints. As presented in Table 6.3, the first step is to calculate the weighted joint distribution. Based on statistical analysis and the '3σ' rule, the normal distribution model and its associated weight for each activity duration are specified through statistical analysis of accumulated system logs. As in the detailed specification of the workflow segment depicted in Table 6.3, the weighted joint distribution of each building block can be derived instantly with their formulas as presented in Section 6.2.1. We obtain the weighted joint distribution as $N(6190,217^2)$ with second as the basic time unit.

The second step is the negotiation process for setting an overall upper bound temporal constraint for this workflow segment. Here, we first illustrate the time-

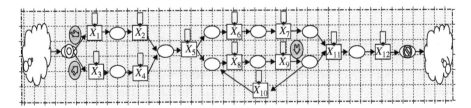

Figure 6.7 Weather forecast scientific cloud workflow segment.

Table 6.3 Specification of the Workflow Segment

Workflow Activities				Joint Distribution	
Activity	Mean	Variance	Weight	Building Blocks	Weighted Joint Distribution
Activity X_1	105	225	0.67	Choice. The	Mean $= 0.67*(105 + 223) +$
				probability for	$0.33*(256 + 358) = 422$
Activity X_2	223	289	0.67	the upper path	Variance $= 0.67^2(225 + 289) +$
Activity X_3	256	529	0.33	is 66.7%, the	$0.33^2(529 + 400) = 331$
Activity X_4	358	400	0.33	lower path is	
				33.3%	
Activity X_5	558	784	1	Sequence	Mean $= 558$; Variance $= 784$
Activity X_6	650	1,089	0	Parallelism and	Mean $= 5*(125 + 285) +$
				iteration. The	$4*594 = 4426$
Activity X_7	230	225	0	probability for	Variance $= 5^2*(64 + 1444) +$
Activity X_8	123	64	5	a single	$4^2*484 = 45444$
Activity X_9	285	1,444	5	iteration is	
Activity X_{10}	594	484	4	25%	
Activity X_{11}	661	529	1	Sequence	Mean $= 661 + 123 = 784$;
Activity X_{12}	123	64	1		Variance $= 529 + 64 = 593$
Overall weight joint distribution				Mean $= 422 + 558 + 4,426 + 784 = 6190$;	
				Variance $= 331 + 784 + 43,444 + 593 = 47,152$	
				The overall weighted joint distribution for the	
				workflow segment $\Rightarrow N(6190, 217^2)$	

oriented negotiation process. We assume that the user's bottom-line confidence of the probability consistency state is 80%. The user starts to present an upper bound temporal constraint of 6250s, based on the weighted joint distribution of $N(6190, 217^2)$ and the cumulative normal distribution function, the service provider can obtain the percentile as $\lambda = 0.28$ and reply with the probability of 61% which is lower than the threshold of 80%. Hence, the service provider advises the user to relax the temporal constraint. Afterwards, for example, the user presents a series of new candidate upper bound temporal constraints one after another, e.g. 6300s, 6360s and 6380s, and the service provider replies with 69%, 78% and 81% as the corresponding temporal consistency states. Since 81% is higher than the 80% minimum threshold, then through a time-oriented negotiation process, the final negotiation result could be an upper bound temporal constraint of $6190 + 0.88*217 = 6380$s with a probability consistency state of 81% where 0.88 is the 81% probability percentile. As for a probability-oriented negotiation process, we assume the user's acceptable latest completion time is 6400s. The user starts to present a probability temporal consistency state of 90%, based on the weighted joint distribution of $N(6190, 217^2)$ and the cumulative normal distribution function; the service provider replies with an upper bound temporal constraint of 6468s which is higher than the threshold. Afterwards, for example, the user presents a series of new candidate probability temporal consistency states one after another, e.g. 88%, 85% and 83%, and the service provider replies with 6445s, 6415s and

Table 6.4 Setting Results

Overall Weight Joint Distribution		
$N(\mu_{SW}, \sigma_{SW}^2) = N(6190, 217^2)$		
Coarse-grained Upper Bound Temporal Constraint		
$U(SW) = 6380$s with 81% consistency and $\lambda = 0.88$		
Fine-grained Upper Bound Temporal Constraints		
$U(X_1) = 108$s	$U(X_2) = 227$s	$U(X_3) = 261$s
$U(X_4) = 362$s	$U(X_5) = 564$s	$U(X_6) = 657$s
$U(X_7) = 233$s	$U(X_8) = 127$s	$U(X_9) = 293$s
$U(X_{10}) = 599$s	$U(X_{11}) = 666$s	$U(X_{12}) = 125$s

6397s as the corresponding temporal consistency states. Since 6397s is lower than the 6400s maximum threshold, through a probability-oriented negotiation process the final negotiation result could be an upper bound temporal constraint of 6397s with a probability temporal consistency state of 83%. Evidently, from this example, with the result of 6380s and 6397s obtained through two different negotiation processes, we can confirm that the setting process is effective no matter which kind of negotiation process is adopted. Furthermore, the final coarse-grained temporal constraints obtained are normally similar if the decision maker is the same user. The setting result of time-oriented negotiation process is presented in Table 6.4.

The third step is to set the fine-grained temporal constrains for each workflow activity with the obtained overall upper bound constraint. As mentioned in Section 6.2.2, the probability-based temporal consistency defines that the probability for each expected activity duration is the same as the probability consistency state of the workflow process. Therefore, take the result obtained through the time-oriented negotiation process for illustration; since the coarse-grained temporal constraint is 6380s with a probability consistency state of 81%, according to Formula (6.2), the fine-grained temporal constraints for each activity can be obtained instantly. Since $\sum_{i=1}^{n} w_i \sigma_i = 412$, $\sqrt{\sum_{i=1}^{n} w_i^2 \sigma_i^2} = 217$ and $\sum_{i=1}^{n} \sigma_i = 250$, the coefficient here is $1 - (412 - 217)/250$ which equals to 0.22. Therefore, for example, the fine-grained upper bound temporal constraint for activity X_1 is $(105 + 0.88 * \sqrt{225} * 0.22) = 108s$ and the constraint for activity X_{12} is $(123 + 0.88 * \sqrt{64} * 0.22) = 125s$. The detailed results are presented in Table 6.4.

Component II

Temporal Consistency Monitoring

7 Temporal Checkpoint Selection and Temporal Verification

After temporal constraints are assigned at build time, the temporal consistency states of workflow execution are to be monitored at run-time. As the first step in the temporal consistency monitoring component, temporal checkpoint selection is to select the activity points where temporal verification is required to be conducted to detect temporal violations. Therefore, the overall time overheads and monetary cost for delivering high temporal QoS are highly related to the number of selected checkpoints along scientific cloud workflow execution. After checkpoint selection, as the second step in the temporal consistency monitoring component, temporal verification is to verify the current temporal consistency states to evaluate the level of the detected temporal violation and obtain the input data for the subsequent actions such as temporal violation handling. Based on the same temporal consistency model, temporal checkpoint selection and temporal verification are usually discussed together for the detection of temporal violations. Therefore, for the ease of discussion and to avoid the redundancies of the technical content, this chapter addresses temporal checkpoint selection together with temporal verification.

This chapter introduces the minimum probability time redundancy-based temporal checkpoint selection strategy and the probability temporal consistency-based temporal verification. This chapter is organised as follows. Section 7.1 presents the specifically related work and problem analysis. Section 7.2 presents the probability time redundancy-based temporal checkpoint selection and temporal verification strategy. Section 7.3 demonstrates the evaluation results.

This chapter is mainly based on our work presented in Ref. [67].

Temporal QoS Management in Scientific Cloud Workflow Systems. DOI: 10.1016/B978-0-12-397010-7.00007-0

7.1 Related Work and Problem Analysis

7.1.1 Related Work

As presented in Chapter 4, checkpoint selection is the first step for monitoring temporal consistency states, and selected checkpoints are the decision points for further actions such as temporal verification and temporal violation handling in the temporal framework. Therefore, checkpoint selection plays a critical role in the whole temporal verification framework since the number of selected checkpoints determines the possible number of times for temporal verification and temporal violation handling [23,67]. Temporal verification is usually conducted after a checkpoint is selected. The original task of temporal verification has two steps. The first step is to check the current temporal consistency state so as to determine whether a specific type of temporal violation has occurred. The second step (after a temporal violation is detected) is to calculate the time deficits (the time delays at the current checkpoint given different temporal constraints) and other run-time information to facilitate the temporal violation handling (i.e. a time-deficit compensation process) of temporal violations.

In recent years, many checkpoint selection strategies, from intuitive rule based to sophisticated model based, have been presented. The work in Ref. [37] takes every workflow activity as a checkpoint. The work in Ref. [69] selects the start activity as a checkpoint and adds a new checkpoint after each decision activity is executed. It also mentions a type of static activity point which is defined by users at the build-time stage. The work in Ref. [24] selects an activity as a checkpoint if its execution time exceeds the maximum duration while the work in Ref. [21] selects an activity as a checkpoint if its execution time exceeds the mean duration. The state-of-the-art checkpoint selection which satisfies the property of necessity and sufficiency is presented in Ref. [22] where minimum time redundancies for SC and WC are defined. For example, an activity point is selected as a WC checkpoint if and only if its execution time is larger than the sum of its mean duration and its minimum WC time redundancy. The comparison result shows that with the measurement of necessity and sufficiency, the one based on minimum time redundancy has outperformed all the other checkpoint selection strategies.

Based on the minimum time redundancy-based checkpoint selection strategies, the work in Refs [21,23] further improves the efficiency of temporal verification by utilising the temporal dependency between temporal constraints. The basic idea is that with temporal dependency, the consistency of some later fixed-time constraints can be deduced from previous ones. Then, based on temporal dependency, CSS_{TD} was presented. With CSS_{TD}, those subsequent fixed-time constraints whose consistency can be deduced from previous ones will no longer take any checkpoints. Accordingly, unlike in other strategies, their verification can be avoided.

7.1.2 Problem Analysis

In order to save the overall cost, the practice of temporal violation handling is to compensate the time deficits by light-weight (small time overheads and monetary cost) violation handling strategies as much as possible instead of conventional expensive heavy-weight temporal violation handling strategies such as resource recruitment and workflow restructure, except for severe temporal violations with excessively large time deficits. Therefore, in this chapter, the range of temporal consistency states where light-weight temporal violation handling is effective needs to be determined first, then statistically recoverable temporal violations can be detected and handled at the early stage before they become severe or unrecoverable (unrecoverable with light-weight temporal violation handling) temporal violations. Unfortunately, a conventional discrete-state-based temporal consistency model with static attributes cannot be employed directly to support statistical analysis.

Given the current multiple-discrete-states-based temporal consistency model [18], at least four types of temporal violations can be defined, namely SC violation, WC violation, WI violation and SI violation. Given the existing state-of-the-art checkpoint selection strategies, we can ensure that, for instance, an SC violation is detected when an SC checkpoint is selected. However, given an SC violation, we still cannot determine whether the detected temporal violation is also a WC, WI or SI violation, or not. Therefore, in the existing work, if an SC checkpoint is selected, it may need to be further verified for WC, WI and SI of all temporal constraints, i.e. three instances of temporal verification for all temporal constraints may be required, if the current temporal violation is an SI violation. Similarly, if a WC checkpoint is selected, two instances of temporal verification for WI and SI may be required, if current temporal violation is an SI violation; if a WI checkpoint is selected, at least one of temporal verification for SI may be required. Therefore, how to decrease the number of temporal verification is a problem to be solved.

7.2 Temporal Checkpoint Selection and Verification Strategy

7.2.1 Probability Range for Statistically Recoverable Temporal Violations with Light-Weight Temporal Violation Handling Strategies

The detailed definition for the probability-based temporal consistency state is presented in Section 6.2 and hence omitted in this chapter. Here, we focus on the introduction of the probability range for statistically recoverable temporal violations. As depicted in Figure 7.1, the effective range for light-weight temporal violation handling is defined as (0.13%, 99.87%) which is represented by the shadowed area. The reason can be explained as follows. Since the maximum and minimum duration for each activity are defined as $D(a_i) = \mu_i + 3\sigma_i$ and $d(a_i) = \mu_i - 3\sigma_i$, respectively, as explained in our hybrid estimation method and proved in Ref. [62], the overall workflow execution time can be estimated with the normal distribution model and has a statistical lower bound of $\mu - 3\sigma$ (with 0.13% consistency) and an upper bound of $\mu + 3\sigma$ (with 99.87% consistency) where μ and σ are the joint normal mean and standard deviation,

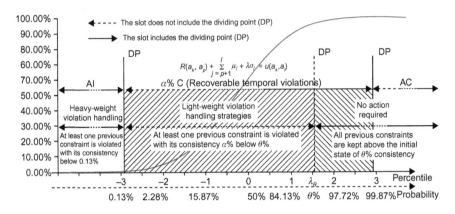

Figure 7.1 Statistically recoverable temporal violations.

respectively, for the durations of all activities included. In practice, at scientific work-flow run-time, temporal violation handling is only triggered in the probability consistency range of (0.13%, θ%) as shown in the area marked with upward diagonal lines in Figure 7.1, while the probability consistency range of (θ%, 99.87%) marked with downward diagonal lines requires no action. Here, the threshold of θ% denotes the minimum acceptable temporal consistency, and it is usually specified through the negotiation between users and service providers for setting local and global temporal constraints [61] (as demonstrated in Section 6.3). In practice, θ% is normally around or above 84.13%, i.e. $\mu + \sigma$. Therefore, if the current temporal consistency of α% (α% Consistency) is larger than θ%, including AC, no action is required since the contract still holds. Otherwise, temporal violation handling is triggered to compensate the time deficit. In other words, a potential temporal violation is deemed as detected when the current temporal consistency state is below the threshold of θ%. However, when α% is below 0.13%, i.e. AI, instead of light-weight temporal violation handling, heavy-weight temporal violation handling strategies such as resource recruitment or workflow restructure (overviewed in Section 9.2) must be implemented since the time remaining before temporal violation is smaller than the minimum completion time that the current scientific workflow system could statistically achieve without an expensive temporal violation handling process. Therefore, AI violations can be regarded as statistically non-recoverable temporal violations.

The probability consistency range where light-weight temporal violation handling is statistically effective is defined as (0.13%, 99.87%). At scientific workflow run-time, based on temporal QoS contracts, light-weight temporal violation handling is only triggered when the probability of current temporal consistency state is within the range of (0.13%, θ%) where θ% is the bottom-line temporal consistency state.

7.2.2   Minimum Probability Time Redundancy

After we have identified the effective probability consistency range for temporal violation handling, the next issue is to determine at which activity point to check for the temporal consistency so that a temporal violation can be detected in the first place. Here, a necessary and sufficient checkpoint selection strategy is presented. First, the definitions of probability time redundancy and minimum probability time redundancy are presented.

Definition 7.1. (Probability Time Redundancy for Single Workflow Activity).

At activity point a_p between a_i and a_j ($i \le j$), let $U(a_i, a_j)$ be of $\beta\%$ C with the percentile of λ_β which is above the threshold of $\theta\%$ with the percentile of λ_θ. Then the probability time redundancy of $U(a_i, a_j)$ at a_p is defined as $PTR(U(a_i, a_j), a_p) = u(a_i, a_j) - [R(a_i, a_p) + \theta(a_{p+1}, a_j)]$. Here, $\theta(a_{p+1}, a_j) = \sum_{k=p+1}^{j}(\mu_k + \lambda_\theta \sigma_k)$.

Definition 7.2. (Minimum Probability Time Redundancy).

Let $U_1, U_2, \ldots, U_N$ be N upper bound constraints and all of them cover a_p. Then, at a_p, the minimum probability time redundancy is defined as the minimum of all probability time redundancies of $U_1, U_2, \ldots, U_N$ and is represented as $MPTR(a_p) = \text{Min}\{PTR(U_s, a_p) | s = 1, 2, \ldots, N\}$.

The purpose of defining minimum probability time redundancy is to detect the earliest possible temporal violations. Based on Definition 7.2, Theorem 7.1 is presented to locate the exact temporal constraint which has the temporal consistency state below the $\theta\%$ bottom line.

Theorem 7.1. At workflow activity point a_p, if $R(a_p) > \theta(a_p) + MPTR(a_{p-1})$, then at least one of the temporal constraints is violated, and it is exactly the one whose time redundancy at a_{p-1} is $MPTR(a_{p-1})$.

Proof. Suppose that $U(a_k, a_l)$ is an upper bound constraint whose probability is above the threshold before execution of a_p ($k < p < l$), it is the one with $MPTR$ (a_{p-1}). Then, according to Definition 7.1, at a_{p-1}, we have $u(a_k, a_l) > R(a_k, a_{p-1}) + \theta(a_p, a_l)$ and here $MPTR(a_{p-1}) = u(a_k, a_l) - R(a_k, a_{p-1}) - \theta(a_p, a_l)$. Now, assume that at activity a_p, we have $R(a_p) > \theta(a_p) + MPTR(a_{p-1})$ which means $R(a_p) > \theta(a_p) + u(a_k, a_l) - R(a_k, a_{p-1}) - \theta(a_p, a_l)$ and that is $u(a_k, a_l) < R(a_p) + R(a_k, a_{p-1}) + \theta(a_p, a_l) - \theta(a_p)$ where the right-hand side equals $R(a_k, a_p) + \theta(a_{p-1}, a_l)$. Since $R(a_k, a_p) + \theta(a_{p-1}, a_l) < R(a_k, a_p) + \theta(a_{p+1}, a_l)$, we have $u(a_k, a_l) < R(a_k, a_p) + \theta(a_{p+1}, a_l)$ and this results in a probability of temporal consistency which is lower than that of $\theta\%$ where $u(a_k, a_l) = R(a_k, a_p) + \theta(a_{p+1}, a_l)$. Therefore, a potential temporal violation is detected and it is exactly the one whose time redundancy at a_{p-1} is $MPTR(a_{p-1})$. Thus, the theorem holds.

7.2.3 Temporal Checkpoint Selection and Temporal Verification Process

Based on Theorem 7.1, we further present Theorem 7.2 which describes our temporal checkpoint selection strategy followed by the proof of its necessity and sufficiency.

Theorem 7.2. (Necessary and sufficient temporal checkpoint selection strategy).

Within the consistency range of ($0.13\% < \alpha\% < 99.87\%$), at activity a_p, if $R(a_p) > \theta(a_p) + MPTR(a_{p-1})$, we select a_p as a temporal checkpoint then we do not select a_p

as a checkpoint. This strategy is of necessity (i.e. all checkpoints selected along workflow execution are necessary) and of sufficiency (i.e. there are no omitted checkpoints).

Proof. According to Theorem 7.1, once we select an activity, say a_p as a checkpoint, there must be at least one temporal constraint which has potential temporal violations detected at a_p and it is exactly the one whose time redundancy at a_{p-1} is $MPTR(a_{p-1})$. That is to say, selecting a_p as a checkpoint is necessary. Thus, the necessity property holds.

With an activity point a_p, we consider it as a checkpoint only if $R(a_p) > \theta(a_p) + MPTR(a_{p-1})$, i.e. $R(a_p) > \theta(a_p) + u(a_i, a_j) - [R(a_i, a_p) + \theta(a_{p+1}, a_j)]$. According to Definition 7.2, if we assume that $u(a_i, a_j)$ is the constraint where minimum probability time redundancy occurs, then $R(a_p) > u(a_i, a_j) - [R(a_i, a_{p-1}) + \theta(a_p, a_j)]$. According to Definition 7.1, Definition 7.2 and the probability consistency range of $(0.13\%, \theta\%)$ where temporal violation handling needs to be triggered, we do not need to select a_p as a checkpoint if $R(a_i, a_p) \leq u(a_i, a_j) - \sum_{k=p}^{j}(\mu_k + \lambda_\theta \sigma_k)$ which means the probability consistency is above $\theta\%$, that is $R(a_p) \leq u(a_i, a_j) - [\theta(a_p, a_j) - R(a_i, a_{p-1})]$ which is $R(a_p) \leq \theta(a_p) + MPTR(a_{p-1})$. Therefore, no checkpoints are omitted. Thus, the sufficiency property holds.

Here, we also adopt the method of DOMTR (Dynamic Obtaining of Minimum Time Redundancy) [22]. Based on some initial values which are set up during the run-time instantiation stage, DOMTR can compute the minimum probability time redundancy on the fly along scientific workflow execution with minimal computation. Based on DOMTR, the computation of our checkpoint selection strategy is basically one or two subtractions or comparisons at each activity covered by one or more upper bound constraints. Therefore, as proved in Ref. [22], the computation cost is basically negligible.

To conclude, our checkpoint selection strategy strictly ensures that a checkpoint is selected only when current temporal consistency is below the minimum acceptable threshold. Meanwhile, since our temporal verification strategy is aware of the effective probability consistency range and can determine the fine-grained levels of temporal violations, it also ensures that statistically the time deficit can be compensated by light-weight temporal violation handling.

7.3   Evaluation

7.3.1   *Experimental Settings*

The SwinDeW-C simulation environment was introduced in Chapter 3 and hence omitted here. The experiment settings are as follows. The process definitions are generated based on the pulsar searching example presented in Section 1.2.1, and the attribute settings are based on historic data for the running of scientific workflow instances [67]. Meanwhile, the experiment settings are extended deliberately for the purpose of exploring a much larger parameter space to evaluate our strategy in general software applications of similar nature in distributed high-performance computing environments.

To evaluate the average performance, 10 independent experiments with different scientific workflow sizes (ranging from 2,000 to 50,000 workflow activities with their mean activity durations between 30 and 3,000 basic time units[1]) are executed 100 times each. All the activity durations are generated by the normal distribution model. The standard deviation is set as 10% of the mean activity duration to represent dynamic system performance. We have also implemented other representative distribution models such as exponential, uniform and a mixture of them (as will be demonstrated in Figure 7.3). Since the experimental results are similar, this section only demonstrates the results with normal distribution.

The constraint setting utilises the strategy introduced in Ref. [62] and the initial probability is set reasonably as 90% to serve as a type of QoS contract between users and service providers which is agreed at scientific workflow build time. Here the initial probability means that a scientific workflow has a 90% probability of finishing on time – in other words, 90% of workflow instances can finish on time. Therefore, in our experiment, we specify the 'satisfactory temporal correctness' as a temporal violation rate below 10% so as to meet the QoS contract. Here, we conduct three rounds of independent experiments where the temporal constraints are set with different normal percentiles of 1.00, 1.15 and 1.28 which denotes the probability of 84.1%, 87.5% and 90.0% for on-time completion without any handling strategies on temporal violations (denoted as COM(1.00), COM(1.15) and COM (1.28)). The average length of the workflow segments is set as 20, which is a moderate size for a workflow sub-process similar to those high-level activities depicted in Figure 1.1.

Meanwhile, to simulate some worse case scenarios, random noises (i.e. a fixed rate of delays at random activities) are also injected to simulate extra delays accordingly along workflow execution due to potential unpredictable causes such as system overload and resource unavailability. For purposes of comparison, four rounds of simulation experiments with different random noise levels of 0%, 10%, 20% and 30% are conducted. Since the standard deviation of activity durations are set as 10% of the mean values, according to the '3σ' rule, there is a slight chance that the noises, i.e. the delays, would exceed 30% of the mean durations [92]. Therefore, we set the upper bound of noises as 30% to investigate the effectiveness of our strategy under extreme situations. As for handling temporal violations, there are many temporal violation handling strategies available (as will be seen in Section 9.2). In our experiments, we choose workflow local rescheduling, which is one of the most widely applied temporal violation handling strategies in the scientific workflow systems, to address the violations of QoS constraints [105,106]. Workflow local rescheduling is to compensate for the time deficit by rescheduling some subsequent activities after the handling point in a local workflow segment to

---

[1] Here, a basic time unit is used for general evaluation purpose. Specifically, for our pulsar searching example, a basic time unit here is more or less equal to a second.

reduce their scheduled execution time (detailed in Section 9.3). In this chapter, since we focus on checkpoint selection and temporal verification, instead of applying a specific workflow rescheduling strategy, a pseudo-rescheduling strategy with a reasonable average time compensation rate (i.e. the reduced rate of the scheduled execution time for the subsequent activities) of 50% is applied to represent the average performance of representative rescheduling strategies [67,105] (detailed in Section 9.5). The size of rescheduled workflow activities, i.e. the number of subsequent activities that need to be rescheduled, is randomly selected up to five which is normally large enough to compensate for time deficit with the given compensation rate. In the real world, not every workflow rescheduling can be successful (e.g. when the current workload is extremely high). Therefore, we set 80% as the success rate for temporal violation handling. CSS_{TD} is applied with default settings as defined in Ref. [23].

7.3.2 Experimental Results

Here, we demonstrate the experiments on checkpoint selection. The number of selected checkpoints is recorded for every experiment. However, for ease of discussion without losing generality, we will only demonstrate the results in COM(1.28), i.e. with a 90% initial probability temporal consistency state. More experimental results and supplementary material can be found online[2]. Since the necessity and sufficiency of our checkpoint selection strategy have already been proved in Section 7.2.3, the experiment here is mainly to verify the effectiveness of our strategy in different system environments. Therefore, additional experiment settings have been implemented. First, we demonstrate the results with different noises. Embedding noises artificially increases the duration of a randomly selected activity. The purpose of embedded noises is to simulate the system environments where unexpected delays often take place. Meanwhile, noises can also simulate estimation errors such as those brought by the two assumptions (e.g. non-normal distribution and correlated activity durations). Here, we conduct four rounds of experiments where the noises are 0%, 10%, 20% and 30%, respectively (i.e. to increase the durations of selected activities by 0%, 10%, 20% and 30%, respectively). A random activity in each workflow segment with the average size of 10 will be selected as the noisy point. Second, we illustrate the results with different distribution models. The purpose of mixed distribution models is to simulate the system environments where many activity durations follow non-normal distributions. Here, we conduct five rounds of experiments where the activity durations are generated by mixed distribution models, for example, 50% of activity durations are generated by normal distribution models, 30% of activity durations are generated by uniform distribution models and the remaining 20% of activity durations are generated by exponential distribution models. Five combinations with different percentages of the three representative distribution models are implemented.

---

[2] http://www.ict.swin.edu.au/personal/xliu/doc/CheckpointSelection.rar

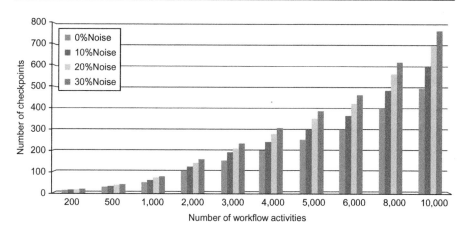

Figure 7.2 Checkpoint selection with different noises.

The results of checkpoint selection with different noises are depicted in Figure 7.2. The number of checkpoints increases accordingly with the growth of workflow size. It is also evident that when the noise is greater, the number of selected checkpoints is also greater. For example, when the number of workflow activities is 6,000, the numbers of checkpoints are 298, 363, 419 and 460 for the noises of 0%, 10%, 20% and 30%, respectively. When the workflow size increases, the differences are even larger. For example, when the number of workflow activities is 10,000, the numbers of checkpoints are 498, 606, 696 and 766 for the noises of 0%, 10%, 20% and 30%, respectively. Note that, given our minimum probability time redundancy-based checkpoint selection strategy, all the selected checkpoints are necessary and sufficient. Therefore, the results actually verify that our strategy can effectively adapt to different system environments. When the system environment becomes more dynamic (with larger noises brought by unexpected delays or estimation errors), more checkpoints are selected to prevent temporal violations.

The checkpoint selection results with different distribution models are depicted in Figure 7.3. The result with 100% normal distribution models is also included as a benchmark. Similarly to Figure 7.2, the number of checkpoints increases accordingly with the increase of workflow size. However, given different combinations with different percentages of the three distribution models, the numbers of selected checkpoints are very close to each other. For example, when the number of workflow activities is 6,000, the numbers of checkpoints are 298, 294, 293, 292, 286 and 287 for 100%Norm, MIX(50%Norm, 30%Uni, 20%Exp), MIX(40%Norm, 40%Uni, 20%Exp), MIX(30%Norm, 40%Uni, 30%Exp), MIX(20%Norm, 40%Uni, 40%Exp) and MIX(10%Norm, 50%Uni, 40%Exp), respectively. The maximum difference is 11. Therefore, even if we regard that all the activity durations follow normal distribution models, the lowest accuracy rate of our checkpoint selection strategy is $1 - (11/298) = 0.96$, i.e. 96%. Specifically, the lowest accuracy rates for the 10 scientific workflows with workflow sizes ranging from 200 to 10,000 are 91%, 93%, 96%, 95%, 96%, 96%, 95%, 96%, 95% and 96%. Therefore, given our checkpoint

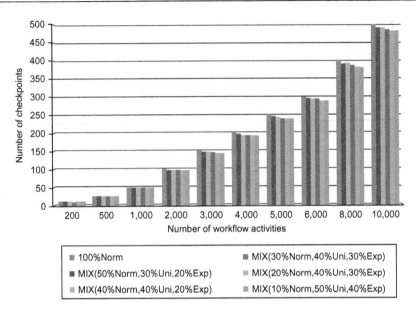

Figure 7.3 Checkpoint selection with different distribution models.

selection strategy, it can be observed that when the workflow size is large enough, the accuracy rate is stable no matter what the actual underlying distribution models are. However, since the real-world system environments normally cannot be simulated exactly by a single distribution model or even several mixed distribution models, the experiments here cannot evaluate our strategy under all possible circumstances but rather by selected representatives. The idea here is to demonstrate that the performance of our strategy will not be affected significantly by the underlying distribution models, although it is built on the normal distribution models.

Component III

Temporal Violation Handling

8 Temporal Violation Handling Point Selection

In scientific cloud workflow systems, temporal violation handling points are those workflow activity points where temporal violation handling strategies are triggered to tackle detected temporal violations. The existing work on temporal verification adopts the philosophy of temporal violation handling required whenever a temporal violation is detected. Therefore, a checkpoint is regarded the same as a temporal violation handling point. However, the probability of self-recovery which utilises the time redundancy of subsequent workflow activities to automatically compensate for the time deficit is ignored and hence would impose a high-temporal violation handling cost. To address such a problem, this book presents a novel adaptive temporal violation handling point selection strategy where the probability of self-recovery is effectively utilised in temporal violation handling point selection to avoid unnecessary handling for temporal violations.

This chapter is organised as follows. Section 8.1 presents the specifically related work and problem analysis. Section 8.2 presents our novel adaptive temporal violation handling point selection strategy. Section 8.3 demonstrates the evaluation results.

This chapter is partly based on our work presented in Ref. [67].

8.1 Related Work and Problem Analysis

8.1.1 Related Work

Due to the dynamic nature of distributed computing infrastructures (e.g. p2p, grid and cloud) and the requirement of QoS, scientific workflow temporal verification

Temporal QoS Management in Scientific Cloud Workflow Systems. DOI: 10.1016/B978-0-12-397010-7.00008-2

has attracted increasing interest in recent years. Many efforts have been dedicated to different tasks involved in temporal verification. As mentioned earlier, a runtime checkpoint selection strategy aims at selecting activity points on the fly to conduct temporal verification so as to improve the efficiency of monitoring large-scale scientific workflows and reduce the computation cost [22]. Meanwhile, to reduce the temporal violation handling cost, multiple-state-based temporal verification is presented to detect multiple fine-grained temporal violations so that different temporal violations (with different levels of time deficits) can be tackled by different temporal violation handling strategies [18].

In recent years, many checkpoint selection strategies, from intuitive rule based to sophisticated model based, have been presented. Most of them are introduced in Section 7.1.1 and hence omitted here. Among them, the state-of-the-art checkpoint selection strategies are those that satisfy the requirements of necessity and sufficiency [22]. As mentioned before, the common philosophy in the studies on temporal verification is that a checkpoint is equal to a temporal violation handling point. Therefore, all these checkpoint selection strategies can be regarded as temporal violation handling point selection strategies. That is, the process of temporal violation handling point selection is actually overlooked in the existing temporal verification and temporal violation handling processes. Therefore, to the best of our knowledge, the issue of temporal violation handling point selection has been neglected so far and not well addressed.

8.1.2 *Problem Analysis*

In the existing work on temporal verification, checkpoint selection is not regarded as an independent task since it normally adopts the philosophy that temporal violation handling should be conducted whenever a temporal violation is detected, i.e. temporal violation handling point selection is the same as checkpoint selection. Accordingly, no matter whether it is a major time deficit of 35 minutes or a minor time deficit of 3 minutes as described in the motivating example in Section 1.2.1, a temporal violation handling is triggered. However, in the real world, it is normally unnecessary to trigger temporal violation handling for a minor time deficit since there is a high probability that it will be automatically compensated for by the time redundancy of the subsequent activities. Therefore, in fact, a checkpoint is not necessarily a temporal violation handling point.

The challenging issue for temporal violation handling point selection is '*how to select the key checkpoints where temporal violation handling is necessary*'. To address such an issue, we need to solve the following two major problems.

1. *How to measure temporal violations in a quantitative fashion*
   In order to reduce the temporal violation handling cost, we need to detect those 'minor' temporal violations with relatively small time deficits. Therefore, it is important that we are able to measure temporal violations in a quantitative fashion. However, the existing temporal consistency models utilise static time attributes such as the maximum and mean durations to define coarse-grained qualitative expressions such as the violation of strong consistency or weak consistency to measure the occurred temporal violations [21,23]. To facilitate the statistical analysis of the time deficit and the time redundancy, it is better to

model activity durations with dynamic variables (following a probability distribution) instead of static time attributes, especially in dynamic system environments [54,61]. Therefore, a temporal consistency model which can facilitate the quantitative measurement of temporal violations is required.

2. *How to decide whether a checkpoint needs to be selected as a temporal violation handling point or not*

Reduction of the temporal violation handling cost is to omit those checkpoints where minor time deficits have a high probability of being compensated for by the expected time redundancy of subsequent activities, i.e. self-recovery. For a necessary and sufficient checkpoint where a temporal violation is detected, the occurred time deficit and the expected time redundancy of subsequent activities after the checkpoint are the basic factors used to decide whether a checkpoint should be selected as a temporal violation handling point or not. Therefore, an effective strategy is required to estimate the probability of self-recovery so as to facilitate temporal violation handling point selection in scientific workflow systems.

8.2 Adaptive Temporal Violation Handling Point Selection Strategy

8.2.1 Probability of Self-Recovery

The details of the probability-based temporal consistency model are presented in Section 6.2 and hence omitted here. Given the probability-based temporal consistency model, we can quantitatively measure different temporal violations based on their probability temporal consistency states. Furthermore, at a specific checkpoint, the occurred time deficit and the expected time redundancy of subsequent activities need to be estimated. They are defined as follows.

Definition 8.1. (Probability Time Deficit).

At activity point a_p, let $U(SW)$ be of $\beta\%$ C with the percentile of λ_β which is below the threshold of $\theta\%$ with the percentile of λ_θ. Then the probability time deficit of $U(SW)$ at a_p is defined as $PTD(U(SW), a_p) = [R(a_1, a_p) + \theta(a_{p+1}, a_n)] - u(SW)$. Here, $\theta(a_{p+1}, a_n) = \sum_{k=p+1}^{n}(\mu_k + \lambda_\theta \sigma_k)$.

Definition 8.2. (Probability Time Redundancy for Single Workflow Segment).

At activity point a_p, let $U(SW)$ be of $\beta\%$ C with the percentile of λ_β which is above the threshold of $\theta\%$ with the percentile of λ_θ. The subsequent activities are defined as those activities from the next activity of the checkpoint, i.e. a_{p+1}, to the end activity of the next temporal constraint, i.e. a_{p+m}. With a segment of size m from a_{p+1} to a_{p+m}, the probability time redundancy of subsequent activities is $PTR(U(SW), (a_{p+1}, a_{p+m}))$ which is equal to $u(SW) - [R(a_1, a_p) + M(a_{p+1}, a_{p+m}) + \theta(a_{p+m+1}, a_n)]$. Here, $M(a_{p+1}, a_{p+m})$ is equal to $\sum_{k=p+1}^{p+m}(\mu_k)$ and $\theta(a_{p+m+1}, a_n)$ is equal to $\sum_{k=p+m+1}^{n}(\mu_k + \lambda_\theta \sigma_k)$.

The probability time deficit is for measuring the occurred time deficit at the current checkpoint. The probability time redundancy is for measuring the expected time redundancy (i.e. the time redundancy between the mean completion time and the temporal constraints) of the subsequent activities at the current checkpoint. For example, at checkpoint a_p, if the temporal constraint for activity a_{p+1} to a_{p+m} is equal to $\mu + \lambda_\theta \sigma$, then the value of $\lambda_\theta \sigma$ is regarded as the expected time redundancy which can be used to compensate for the occurred time deficit. Based on the probability time deficit and the probability time redundancy, the probability of self-recovery is defined as follows.

Definition 8.3. (Probability of Self-Recovery).

For activity point a_p which is covered by $U(SW)$, given the probability time deficit (denoted as $PTD(a_p)$) and the probability time redundancy (denoted as $PTR(a_p)$), the probability of self-recovery, i.e. the probability that $PTD(a_p)$ can be compensated for by $PTR(a_p)$, is defined as:

$$P(T) = \frac{1}{\sqrt{2\pi}} \int_{-\infty}^{T} e^{\frac{-x^2}{2}}, \quad \text{where } T = \frac{PTR(a_p) - PTD(a_p)}{PTD(a_p)}$$

If, without any prior knowledge, it is difficult to decide which probability distribution model that T fits, then in this chapter, we assume that T follows a standard normal distribution[1], i.e. $N(0,1)$ with the expected value of 0 and the standard deviation of 1. It is obvious that the larger the difference between $PTR(a_p)$ and $PTD(a_p)$, the higher the probability for self-recovery. For example, according to Definition 8.3, if $PTR(a_p)$ is equal to $PTD(a_p)$, i.e. T is equal to 0, the probability for self-recovery is 50%. If $PTR(a_p)$ is twice as large as $PTD(a_p)$, i.e. T is equal to 1, the probability for self-recovery is 84.13% [92]. Note that in practice, historical data can be employed to discover and modify the actual probability distribution models. Nevertheless, the strategy presented in this chapter can be applied in a similar manner.

8.2.2 Temporal Violation Handling Point Selection Strategy

After the probability of self-recovery is defined, a probability threshold is required. The probability threshold can be regarded as the minimum confidence for skipping temporal violation handling on a selected checkpoint while still retaining satisfactory temporal correctness. Given a probability threshold, a temporal violation handling point selection rule is defined as follows.

Temporal Violation Handling Point Selection Rule

At activity a_p, with the probability of self-recovery $P(T)$ and the probability threshold PT ($0 < PT < 1$), the rule for temporal violation handling point selection is as follows: if $P(T) > PT$, then the current checkpoint is not selected as a handling point; otherwise, the current checkpoint is selected as a handling point.

The probability threshold PT is an important parameter in the temporal violation handling point selection rule and it needs to be defined to facilitate violation handling

---

[1] Note that we have tested our strategy with other distribution models such as exponential, uniform and a mixture of them. The results are similar.

point selection at workflow run-time. However, whether self-recovery will be successful or not can only be determined after the execution of the subsequent activities. It is difficult, if not impossible, to specify the optimal probability threshold which can select the minimal number of handling points while maintaining satisfactory temporal correctness. To address this problem, we borrow the idea from adaptive testing where the new testing cases are generated based on the knowledge of previous testing cases [25]. In our strategy, the probability threshold can start from any moderate initial values, for example, 0.3 or 0.5, and it is then adaptively modified based on the results of previous temporal violation handling along scientific workflow execution. Therefore, the initial threshold has limited impact on the effectiveness of our strategy. The process of adaptive modification for *PT* is described as follows.

Adaptive Modification Process for Probability Threshold

Given current probability threshold PT ($0 < PT < 1$) and checkpoint a_p, i.e. a temporal violation is detected at a_p, PT is updated as $PT*(1 + \gamma)$. Afterwards, based on our handling point selection rule, if a_p is not selected as a handling point, then PT is updated as $PT*(1 - \gamma)$; otherwise, PT remains unchanged. Here, γ stands for the update rate which is a small percentile.

The adaptive modification process is to increase the probability threshold PT, i.e. the probability of temporal violation handling, where temporal violation handling is triggered; or to decrease PT where temporal violation handling is skipped if self-recovery applies. As shown in Table 8.1, our temporal violation handling point selection strategy is to apply the adaptive modification process for probability threshold to the handling point selection rule.

The input parameters for the strategy include the necessary and sufficient checkpoint, the probability time deficit, the probability time redundancy and the probability threshold. Since handling point selection is based on the results of the state-of-the-art checkpoint selection strategy, i.e. the minimum time redundancy-based checkpoint selection strategy where the time overhead is negligible, the computation of the probability time redundancy according to Definition 8.2 can be included in the checkpoint selection process [67]. Therefore, since PT is a variant, the only extra cost for computing the input parameters is for the probability time deficit according to Definition 8.1. After the input parameters are specified, the current probability of self-recovery is obtained according to Definition 8.3 and compared with the adaptively updated probability threshold to further decide whether the current checkpoint needs to be selected as a temporal violation handling point or not. The time overhead for our temporal violation handling point selection strategy can be viewed as negligible since it requires only several steps of simple calculation. In the next section, we will evaluate the performance of our strategy comprehensively.

8.3 Evaluation

In the existing work, temporal violation handling point selection is regarded the same as checkpoint selection; hence the existing state-of-the-art checkpoint

Table 8.1 Adaptive Temporal Violation Handling Point Selection Strategy

Adaptive Random Temporal Violation Handling Point Selection Strategy

Input	A necessary and sufficient checkpoint a_p The maximum probability time deficit $MPTD(a_p)$ The minimum probability time redundancy $MPTR(a_p)$ The probability threshold for auto-recoveiy PT The result of last temporal adjustment $Success \in (True, False)$
Output	True or False as a temporal violation handling point
Step 1	Adaptive adjustment of PT

if (*Success* = *True*)

　　　$PT = PT\,(1+0.1*r)$　 // *if the last temporal violation handling is successful, the current probability threshold is increased according to a predefined speed*

else

　　　$PT = PT\,(1-0.1*r)$　 // *if failed, decreased according to a predefined speed*

Step 2	Temporal violation handling point selection

$$P = F(MPTR(a_p) - MPTD(a_p)) = F(T) = \frac{1}{\sqrt{2x}} \int_{-\infty}^{T} \ell^{\frac{-x^2}{2}}$$

if (*P*>*PT*)

　　　a_p is not selected as a violation handling point　 // *if the current probability of self-recovery is larger than the probability threshold, temporal violation handling is skipped*

else

　　　a_p is selected as an adjustment point　 //*temporal violation handling is required*

selection strategy (with the minimum number of selected checkpoints) CSS_{TD} [23] is implemented as the benchmark for comparison with ours. The detailed description for CSS_{TD} and its performance (which was better than the other eight representative strategies) are omitted in this chapter but can be found in Ref. [23]. In addition, to evaluate the effectiveness of our adaptive strategy, a pure random handling point selection strategy denoted as RA is also implemented. RA selects handling points at every necessary and sufficient checkpoint in a pure random fashion. The selection rule of RA is as follows: at a necessary and sufficient checkpoint a_p, a random value $R(0 < R < 1)$ is first generated. Afterwards, R is compared with the predefined fixed confidence threshold FT ($0 < FT < 1$), if R is larger than FT, then a_p is selected as a handling point. Otherwise, a_p is not selected as a handling point. In RA, the fixed confidence threshold FT actually decides how many of the checkpoints will be selected as handling points. For example, if FT is set as 0.9, then a total of $1 - 0.9 = 0.1$, i.e. 10% of the checkpoints will be selected as violation handling points while the others will be skipped without temporal violation handling.

Table 8.2 Experimental Settings

Scientific cloud workflows	The scientific workflow size: from 2,000 to 50,000 workflow activities
	Activity durations: all activity durations follow the normal distribution model. The mean duration is randomly selected from 30 to 3,000 time units, and the standard deviation is set as 10% of its mean
	Temporal constraints: the initial build-time probability for deadlines are set as 60% according to Ref. [62]
	Workflow segments: the average length of the workflow segments for subsequent activities is set as 20
	Random noises: the duration of one selected activity in each workflow segment is increased by 5%, 15% or 25% of its mean in different rounds
Exception handling	Exception handling strategy: workflow local rescheduling
	The size of rescheduled workflow activities: randomly selected as 3−5
	Time compensation rate: the time compensation rate for temporal adjustment is set as 50%
	Success rate: the success rate for temporal adjustment is set as 80%
CSS_{TD}	Default values as defined in Ref. [21]
RT	The fixed confidence threshold: FT is set as 0.9, i.e. select 10% from the total checkpoints as adjustment points in a pure random fashion
AD	The update rate: γ is initially set as 5 and gradually decreased to 0.5 as explained in Section 8.2

As shown in Table 8.2, the experimental settings are as follows. The process definitions are generated based on the pulsar searching example presented in Section 1.2.1 and the attribute settings are based on historic data for the running of scientific workflow instances [67]. Meanwhile, the experiment settings are extended deliberately for the purpose of exploring a much larger parameter space to evaluate our strategy in general software applications of a similar nature in distributed high-performance computing environments.

To evaluate the average performance, 10 independent experiments with different scientific workflow sizes (ranging from 2,000 to 50,000 workflow activities with their mean activity durations between 30 and 3,000 time units) are executed 100 times each. All the activity durations are generated by the normal distribution model. The standard deviation is set as 10% of the mean activity duration to represent dynamic system performance. We have also implemented other representative distribution models such as exponential, uniform and a mixture of them. Since the experimental results are similar, this chapter demonstrates only the results with normal distribution.

The constraint setting utilises the strategy introduced in Ref. [62], and the initial probability is set reasonably as 90% to serve as a type of QoS contract between users and service providers which is agreed at scientific workflow build time. Here the initial probability means that a scientific workflow has a 90% probability of finishing on time or, in other words, 90% workflow instances can finish on time. Therefore, in our experiment, we specify the 'satisfactory temporal correctness' as a temporal violation rate below 10% so as to meet the QoS contract. The average length of the workflow segments is set as 20 which is a moderate size for a workflow sub-process similar to those high-level activities depicted in Figure 1.1. Meanwhile, to simulate some worst-case scenarios, random noises (i.e. a fixed rate of delays at random activities) are also injected to simulate extra delays accordingly along workflow execution due to potential unpredictable causes such as system overload and resource unavailability. For purposes of comparison, four rounds of simulation experiments with different random noise levels of 0%, 5%, 15% and 25% are conducted. Since the standard deviations of activity durations are set as 10% of the mean values, according to the '3σ' rule, there is a slight chance that the noises, i.e. the delays, would exceed 30% of the mean durations [92]. Therefore, we set the upper bound of noises as 25% to investigate the effectiveness of our strategy under extreme situations. There are many temporal violation handling strategies available as will be introduced in Chapter 9. In our experiments, similar to the settings in Section 7.3.1, we use pseudo-workflow local rescheduling with a reasonable average time compensation rate of 50% [67,105]. The size of rescheduled workflow activities is randomly selected up to 5 which is normally large enough to compensate for time deficits with the given compensation rate. The success rate for temporal violation handling is set as 80%. CSS_{TD} is applied with default values as defined in Ref. [23]. The fixed confidence threshold for RA is set as 0.9 (i.e. select 10%) so as to be comparable to our strategy, denoted as AD. The initial probability threshold and the update rate for our strategy are set as 0.5 (midrange initially) and 5% (a small percentile), respectively. This is a moderate and reasonable setting when there is no prior knowledge. Additionally, to reflect the effectiveness of temporal violation handling, the results of workflow execution under the natural condition without temporal violation handling (denoted as NIL) are also presented.

Here, before we demonstrate the experiments on temporal violation handling point selection in detail, we present an overview of the results of the cost for handling temporal violations in scientific workflow systems. The two representative temporal violation handling strategies investigated in our system are workflow rescheduling and extra resource recruitment. Workflow rescheduling is to compensate the time deficit by optimising the current activity-resource assignment. The major overhead involved in workflow rescheduling includes activity transfer (data and activity definitions) between resources, and the computation overhead of the rescheduling strategy itself. In our SwinDeW-C scientific workflow system, for a typical workflow rescheduling scenario (with around 200 activities and 10 resources), the average overhead for activity transfer is around 2 minutes and the computation overhead is around 0.2 minutes [67]. As for extra resource recruitment, this is to compensate the time deficit by employing additional resources for the violated workflow instances at run-time. Its major overhead includes the set-up

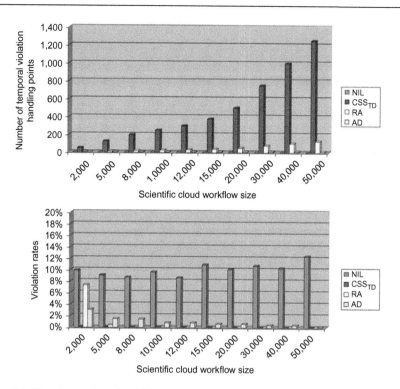

Figure 8.1 Experimental results (Noise = 0%).

time for new resources and the task transfer time. For a typical resource recruitment scenario (adding one new resource), the normal set-up time for a single resource is several minutes (like the Amazon EC2 Reserved Instances: http://aws.amazon.com/ec2/reserved-instances/), and the activity transfer time (for fewer than five activities in a local workflow segment) is around 0.3 minutes. Furthermore, to give a direct view of the savings on the total temporal violation handling cost, we record the reduced overhead for the 10 test cases in each round of the experiment. For example, if we specify the basic time unit as one second, the results have shown that for a large-scale scientific workflow (with over 10,000 activities and around 300 violations in the 0% noise case), the reduced overhead is around 15 hours for workflow rescheduling strategy, and around 40 hours for resource recruitment strategy. As indicated earlier, since the overhead for our handling point selection strategy is negligible, the amount of reduced overhead for temporal violation handling is significant. More details can be referred online[2].

Here we demonstrate the four rounds of experiments in detail. The experiment results with 0% noise are depicted in Figure 8.1. The case of 0% noise should be the norm in the real world when the system is under a reasonably smooth and

---

[2] http://www.ict.swin.edu.au/personal/xliu/doc/HandlingPointSelection.rar

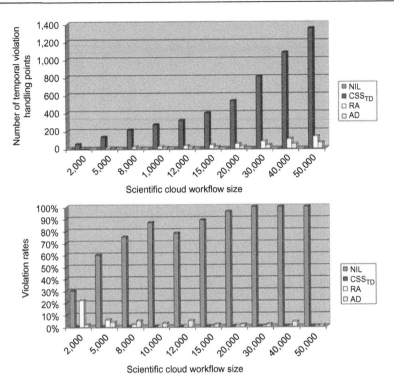

Figure 8.2 Experimental results (Noise = 5%).

stable condition. However, even in such a normal circumstance, the number of checkpoint (i.e. handling points) selected by CSS_{TD} increases rapidly with the growth of scientific workflow size. For RA, since the fixed confidence threshold is set as 0.9, it chooses 10% of the handling points selected by CSS_{TD}. NIL does not select any handling points. As for our adaptive handling point selection strategy, AD, it selects a very small portion, i.e. 1.3%, of those selected by CSS_{TD}. This is a significant reduction, i.e. 98.7% of the temporal violation handling cost over CSS_{TD} in terms of cost-effectiveness. Meanwhile, we compare the violation rate of each strategy. The violation rate of NIL is around 10% as expected due to the agreed QoS contract set at build time. As for CSS_{TD}, the violation rate can be kept close to 0%. Except for a small scientific workflow with a size of 2,000 where RA and AD have violation rates of around 7% and 3%, respectively, due to limited opportunities for temporal violation handling, all the others are very small with close to 0% violations. In fact, for AD, the violation rate decreases whilst the workflow size increases.

The results with 5% random noise are depicted in Figure 8.2. The number of selected handling points by AD is around 5.0% (namely 95.0% cost reduction) of CSS_{TD}. In terms of temporal violation, the violation rate for NIL is much higher than for others and increases to over 90% when the workflow size is larger than

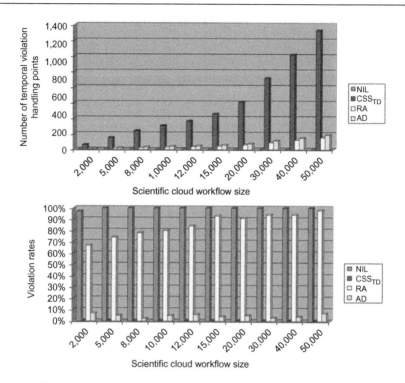

Figure 8.3 Experimental results (Noise = 15%).

15,000. The violation rate for CSS_{TD} is still kept close to 0%. As for RA, the violation rate is generally higher than the previous round. But when the workflow size increases, the violation rate decreases since temporal violation handling is conducted many more times. In contrast, our strategy AD behaves stably and maintains an average temporal violation rate of around just 3.0%.

Figure 8.3 shows the results with 15% random noise. AD adaptively selects more handling points than that in the previous round due to the increase of the noises. The number of handling points selected by AD is very close to that of RA when the scientific workflow size is small. But when it becomes larger, their differences increase. On average, the number of handling points selected by AD is 25% more than that of RA, i.e. around 12.5% (namely 87.5% cost reduction) of CSS_{TD}. In terms of temporal violation, the violation rate for NIL is close to 100% for all the cases. In contrast, CSS_{TD} can still keep the violation rate close to 0%. The violation rate for RA is above 70% and increases to over 90% when the workflow size is above 30,000. As for AD, since it can adapt to the dynamic system performance, the violation rate is still stable with an average violation rate only increasing to around 4.8%.

Figure 8.4 shows the results with a rather extreme 25% random noise. The number of selected handling points by AD is generally larger, actually with an average

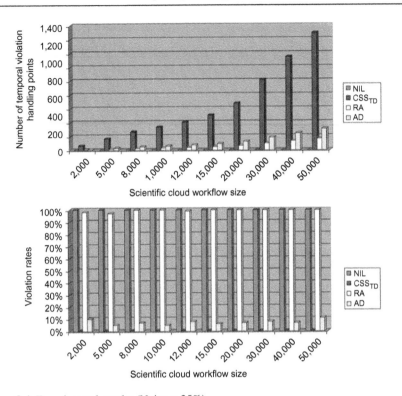

Figure 8.4 Experimental results (Noise = 25%).

of 85% more than that of *RA*, i.e. around 18.5% (namely 81.5% cost reduction) of CSS_{TD}. In terms of temporal violation, the violation rate for *NIL* is still close to 100% for all the cases. CSS_{TD} can still keep the violation rate close to 0% at the cost of a large amount of temporal violation handling. The violation rate for *RA* is now close to 100% for most cases. *AD* can still behave stably with an average temporal violation rate of around 7.4% under such extreme conditions.

As shown in Figure 8.5, against the benchmark of CSS_{TD}, the cost reduction rates of our strategy are around 98.7% for 0% noise, 95.0% for 5% noise, 87.5% for 15% noise and 81.5% for 25% noise, respectively. The corresponding violation rates are close to 0% for 0% noise, 3.0% for 5% noise, 4.8% for 15% noise and 7.4% for 25% noise, respectively, all below 10% violation rate which denotes the satisfactory temporal correctness. In particular, the results for 0% noise with the 98.7% cost reduction rate and the close to 0% violation rate is very promising in terms of cost-effectiveness and temporal correctness because this is the normal circumstance. In overall terms, the results effectively demonstrate that our adaptive temporal violation handling point selection strategy can significantly reduce the temporal violation handling cost while maintaining satisfactory temporal correctness, i.e. lower than the temporal violation rate of 10% which is the agreed QoS contract between users and service providers before workflow execution. Meanwhile, we have also checked

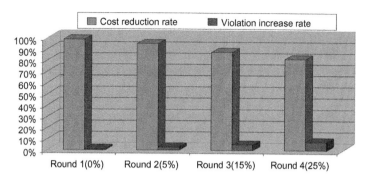

Figure 8.5 Cost reduction rate versus violation increase rate.

the time overruns in every workflow instance with our *AD* strategy. The results show that the time overruns are often very small in comparison to the overall temporal constraint which can most likely be tolerated by users.

To summarise, with fundamental requirements of temporal correctness and cost-effectiveness, we can conclude that our strategy performs much better than other representative temporal violation handling point selection strategies with different system performance varying from smooth to non-smooth situations.

9 Temporal Violation Handling

Temporal violation handling is the key of the last component in our temporal framework for scientific cloud workflow systems. Clearly, whether a detected temporal violation can be recovered or not depends mainly on the performance of temporal violation handling strategies employed in the system. Meanwhile, since the time overheads and monetary cost for temporal violation handling strategies are usually much more expensive than those of its precedent steps such as checkpoint selection and temporal verification, cost-effective temporal violation handling strategies are required to be employed or designed to reduce the overall cost of the temporal framework.

This chapter is organised as follows. Section 9.1 introduces the specifically related work and problem analysis. Section 9.2 presents an overview of temporal violation handling strategies for both statistically recoverable and non-recoverable temporal violations. Section 9.3 presents a novel general two-stage local workflow rescheduling strategy which utilises metaheuristics algorithms to handle statistically recoverable temporal violations. Furthermore, two representative metaheuristics algorithms, GA and ACO, are implemented as two specific candidate strategies. Section 9.4 presents three levels of temporal violations and their corresponding handling strategies which are implemented in our temporal framework. Section 9.5 comprehensively compares the performance of GA- and ACO-based rescheduling strategies. Section 9.6 demonstrates the overall performance of the three-level temporal violation handling strategy and conducts cost analysis.

This chapter is mainly based on our work presented in Refs [60,63,64,66,67,99].

9.1 Related Work and Problem Analysis

9.1.1 Related Work

The work in Ref. [88] introduces five types of workflow exceptions where temporal violations can be classified into deadline expiry. The work in Ref. [87] presents three alternate courses of recovery action: no action (*NIL*), rollback (*RBK*) and compensation (*COM*). *NIL*, which entirely counts on the automatic recovery of the system itself, is normally not considered 'risk-free'. As for *RBK*, unlike handling conventional system function failures, it normally causes extra delays and makes the current temporal violations even worse. In contrast, *COM*, or time-deficit compensation, is a suitable approach for handling temporal violations. The work in Ref. [18]

Temporal QoS Management in Scientific Cloud Workflow Systems. DOI: 10.1016/B978-0-12-397010-7.00009-4

presents a *TDA* strategy which compensates current time deficits by utilising the expected time redundancy of subsequent activities. Here, the time deficit is the amount of time that has been delayed given the actual durations and the temporal constraints, while the time redundancy is the expected extra time between the mean durations and temporal constraints. Therefore, the actual role of *TDA* is to verify the possibility of auto-compensation by future workflow segments. However, since the time deficit is not truly reduced by *TDA*, this strategy can only postpone the violations of local constraints on some local workflow segments but is ineffective on global constraints, for example, the final deadlines. Therefore, in this chapter, to handle both local and global temporal violations, those strategies which can indeed reduce the time deficits need to be investigated. Besides many others, one of the compensation processes that is often employed and can actually make up the time deficit is to amend the schedule of the workflow activities, i.e. workflow rescheduling [106].

Workflow rescheduling, such as local rescheduling (which deals with the mapping of underling resources to workflow activities within specific local workflow segments), is normally triggered by the violation of QoS constraints [30]. Workflow scheduling as well as workflow rescheduling are classical NP-complete problems [28]. Therefore, many heuristic and metaheuristic algorithms are proposed [7,95,105]. The work in Ref. [105] has presented a systematic overview of workflow scheduling algorithms for scientific grid computing. The major grid workflow scheduling algorithms have been classified into two basic categories: best-effort-based scheduling and QoS-constraint-based scheduling. Best-effort-based scheduling attempts to minimise the execution time with ignoring other factors such as cost, while QoS-constraint-based scheduling attempts to minimise performance under important QoS constraints, for example, makespan minimisation under budget constraints or cost minimisation under deadline constraints. Many heuristic methods such as Minimum Completion Time, Min−Min and Max−Min have been proposed for best-effort-based scheduling [95]. As for QoS-constraint-based scheduling, some metaheuristic methods such as GA and SA (Simulated Annealing) have been proposed and exhibit satisfactory performance [105]. In recent years, ACO, a type of optimisation algorithm inspired by the foraging behaviour of real ants in the wild, has been adopted to address large complex scheduling problems and has proven to be quite effective in many distributed and dynamic resource environments, such as parallel processor systems and grid workflow systems [27]. The work in Ref. [26] presents an ACO approach to address scientific workflow scheduling problems with various QoS requirements such as reliability constraints, makespan constraints and cost constraints. A balanced ACO algorithm for job scheduling is proposed in Ref. [13] which can balance the entire system load while trying to minimise the makespan of a given set of jobs. For handling temporal violations in scientific cloud workflow systems, both time and cost need to be considered, although time has a priority over cost since we focus more on reducing the time deficits during the compensation process. Therefore, QoS-constraint-based scheduling algorithms are better choices for handling temporal violations. An ACO-based local workflow rescheduling strategy is proposed by us in Ref. [60] for handling temporal violations in scientific workflows.

9.1.2 Problem Analysis

Two fundamental requirements for handling temporal violations are *automation* and *cost-effectiveness*.

1. *Automation*: Due to the complex nature of scientific applications and their distributed running environments such as grid and cloud, a large number of temporal violations may often be expected in scientific workflows. Besides, scientific workflow systems are designed to be highly automatic to conduct large-scale scientific processes, human interventions which are normally of low efficiency should be avoided as much as possible, especially during workflow run-time [32]. Therefore, similar to dynamic checkpoint selection and temporal verification strategies [21], temporal violation handling strategies should be designed to automatically tackle a large number of temporal violations and relieve users from the heavy workload of handling those violations.

2. *Cost-effectiveness*: Handling temporal violations is to reduce, or ideally remove, the delays of workflow execution by temporal violation handling strategies with the sacrifice of additional cost which consists of both monetary cost and time overheads. Conventional temporal violation handling strategies such as resource recruitment and workflow restructure are usually very expensive [10,46,77,87]. The cost for recruiting new resources (e.g. the cost for service discovery and deployment, the cost for data storage and transfer) is normally very large during workflow run-time in distributed computing environments [77]. As for workflow restructure, it is usually realised by the amendment of local workflow segments or temporal QoS contracts, i.e. modifying scientific workflow specifications by human decision makers [61]. However, due to budget (i.e. monetary cost) limits and temporal constraints, these heavy-weight strategies (with large monetary cost and/or time overheads) are usually too costly to be practical. To avoid these heavy-weight strategies, recoverable violations (in comparison to severe temporal violations which can be regarded as non-recoverable in practice) need to be identified first and then handled by light-weight strategies (with small monetary cost and/or time overheads) in a cost-effective fashion.

9.2 Overview of Temporal Violation Handling Strategies

As introduced in Section 7.2.1 with Figure 7.1, given the probability-based temporal consistency model, temporal violations occurring in scientific cloud workflow systems can be classified as statistically recoverable and non-recoverable temporal violations. Statistically recoverable temporal violations are usually the result of minor delays in workflow activity durations caused by the dynamic performance of underlying cloud services. Statistically non-recoverable temporal violations are usually brought about by major delays caused by some serious technical problems such as machine breakdown and network outage. These problems are normally controlled by effective system design and thus happen very infrequently (e.g. outside the '3σ' probability range); in other words, the frequency of statistically non-recoverable temporal violations is kept very low in a running scientific cloud workflow system. However, to deliver high temporal QoS, temporal violation handling strategies for both recoverable and non-recoverable temporal violations are required. In this chapter, we introduce some representative temporal violation handling strategies for dealing with both recoverable and non-recoverable temporal violations.

9.2.1 Temporal Violation Handling of Statistically Recoverable Temporal Violations

Some common temporal violation handling strategies for handling recoverable temporal violations include *NIL* (no action), *TDA*, workflow rescheduling and hybrid strategies.

NIL (no action): *NIL* is not an actual temporal violation handling strategy but works well in the dynamic system environments where minor delays often take place. The reason is the same as the motivation for our adaptive temporal violation handling point selection strategy, i.e. the probability for self-recovery, since some minor delays can probably be automatically compensated by the saved execution time of the subsequent workflow activities. However, the *NIL* strategy cannot perform alone since there is the risk of not handling minor temporal violations. Therefore, it should be accompanied by, for example, our adaptive temporal violation handling point selection strategy to ensure its effectiveness. Otherwise, it is not applicable for 'risk-free' system management.

TDA: *TDA* is based on an idea similar to *NIL* but with a more active action which allocates the existing time deficit proportionally to the subsequent workflow activities. The purpose of such an action is to postpone the current temporal violation and determine the time deficit which should be compensated by each of the subsequent workflow activities so as to recover the current temporal violations. Given the allocated time deficit, some local optimisation may be applied to decrease the current scheduled execution time. However, *TDA* alone does not involve any time-deficit compensation strategies. Therefore, similar to *NIL*, *TDA* is not effective for handling temporal violations if performed without real-time deficit compensation processes.

Workflow rescheduling: workflow rescheduling is to optimise the current workflow scheduling plan to adapt to the changes of the current system environments, especially the violation of temporal constraints. Different from workflow scheduling, which aims to optimise some global objectives such as cost and makespan for the entire workflow instance, workflow rescheduling normally gives priority to some specific workflow activities so as to optimise some local objectives such as decreasing the cost or makespan of a local workflow segment. Therefore, workflow rescheduling usually targets local optimised solutions. There are many workflow rescheduling strategies and among them the most popular ones are metaheuristics-based workflow rescheduling strategies [7,105]. In this chapter, GA- and ACO-based rescheduling strategies will be discussed in detail.

Hybrid strategies: as analysed above, some light-weight temporal violation handling strategies such as *NIL* and *TDA* cannot perform well without the complementary of other strategies which can indeed compensate time deficits. Therefore, some hybrid strategies are designed. For example, the hybrid strategy of *TDA* and workflow rescheduling strategy, or specifically *TDA*- and ACO-based workflow rescheduling strategy (TDA + ACO for short), is proposed by us in Ref. [63] to deal with major but recoverable temporal violations. The experimental results in Ref. [63] have shown that the performance of the TDA + ACO is better than the standalone TDA and also the standalone ACO-based workflow rescheduling strategy.

9.2.2   Temporal Violation Handling of Statistically Non-Recoverable Temporal Violations

Some common temporal violation handling strategies for handling non-recoverable temporal violations include resource recruitment, stop and restart, processor swapping and workflow restructure.

Resource recruitment: resource recruitment adds new resources at workflow run-time. It is a very common solution for speeding up workflow execution so as to compensate existing time delays. Adding a new resource is also very commonly used to handle temporal violations. For example, in a scientific cloud computing environment, the underlying cloud infrastructure can provide unlimited scalable resource on demand at workflow run-time. Therefore, we can add a new resource (i.e. a new virtual machine, VM) to execute the local workflow segment for the violated workflow instances. In that case, these workflow activities can be given higher priority (to decrease the waiting time) and/or higher execution speed (to decrease the execution time), and hence the existing time deficits can be compensated. To realise that, all the computation tasks and input data of these activities need to be reallocated to the new resources.

Additional monetary cost and time overheads are required for adding a new resource at workflow run-time. The monetary cost for adding a new resource in the pay-for-usage cloud computing environment is mainly equal to the transfer cost since it is normally free to set up new resources; the total time overheads consist of the transfer time for the data and the set-up time for a new service which is normally around several minutes as in Amazon Elastic Compute Cloud (EC2, http://aws.amazon.com/ec2/) depending on the load of the system and network.

Stop and restart: stop and restart consist of two basic steps. The stop step is to stop the execution at the current checkpoint and store all the running data. The restart step is to restart the application at a new set of resources. Although the strategy is very flexible, the natural stop, migrate and restart approach to rescheduling can be expensive: each migration event may involve large volume of data transfers. Moreover, restarting the application can incur expensive start-up costs, and significant application modifications may be required (with human interventions) for specialised restart code. As demonstrated in Ref. [30], the overhead for this strategy includes at least the following aspects: resource selection, performance modelling, computing resource overhead, application start, checkpoint reading. Among them, the time for reading checkpoints dominates the rescheduling overhead, as it involves moving data across the Internet and redistributing data to more processors. According to their experiments, the average overhead for the strategy is around 500 seconds.

Processor swapping: the basic idea of processor swapping is as follows: applications are launched with the reservations of more machines than actually used at workflow build time; and then at run-time, slower machines in the active set are constantly monitored and periodically swapped with faster machines in the inactive set. This strategy is also generic and intuitive, but it is only effective when there is a sufficient number of free resources available in the system. Compared with stop and restart, the overhead of processor swapping is much lower. However, the cost for reserving a large number of resources is very high. For example in Amazon EC2, the price for reserving a high-memory or high-CPU instance is around \$0.5 per hour. Therefore, the cost for a processor swapping strategy by reserving a large number of resources in scientific workflow systems is very high.

Workflow restructure: under the condition in which severe violations take place, one of the last resorts is workflow restructure which may modify the current QoS contracts by relaxing some of the QoS constraints or even abandoning some less important workflow sub-processes. This strategy will inevitably involve significant human interventions such as negotiation between users and service providers, and human decision-making processes to determine the corresponding actions. These processes are usually very time consuming not only because of their own complexities but also because of the involvement of human participants. Furthermore, since workflow restructure brings the modification of the current service contracts or even the sacrifice of workflow execution results, penalties would normally be applied to service providers.

To conclude, the temporal violation handling strategies for non-recoverable temporal violations are usually very expensive with large monetary cost and huge time overheads. Also, since they normally require human interventions, they can only be conducted in a manual or semi-automatic fashion and hence mean a heavy workload for users and service providers. Given the fundamental requirements of *automation* and *cost-effectiveness* for handling temporal violations in scientific cloud workflow systems, these heavy-weight temporal violation handling strategies should be avoided as much as possible except in cases of non-recoverable temporal violations.

9.3 A Novel General Two-Stage Local Workflow Rescheduling Strategy for Recoverable Temporal Violations

9.3.1 Description of the General Strategy

Given the two fundamental requirements of *automation* and *cost-effectiveness*, the temporal violation handling strategies that we mainly investigate in this chapter are metaheuristics-based workflow rescheduling algorithms. With metaheuristics-based rescheduling algorithms, temporal violations are tackled by rescheduling the current Task-to-Resource assignment. Note that in cloud computing environments, computing resources are generally delivered as VMs. Therefore, in this chapter, Task-to-Resource assignment and Task-Resource list are interchangeable with Task-to-VM assignment or Task-VM list, respectively. For workflow rescheduling, the following two challenges need to be considered: (1) the balance between the handling of temporal violations and the on-time completion of other workflow instances; (2) the suitable size of the Task-Resource list for cost-effective rescheduling. The reason we do not consider heuristics-based scheduling algorithms in this scenario is mainly as follows:

1. Heuristics-based scheduling algorithms can only optimise one objective at a time. Meanwhile, they are based on local optimisation in which they can choose the best

---

Strategy: Two-Stage Local Workflow Rescheduling

Input: Time deficit detected at activity a_p $TD(a_p)$;

Integrated Task-Resource list $L\{(a_i, R_j) \mid i = p + 1,...p + n, j = 1,2,..K\}$;

DAG task graphs $DAG\{G_i \mid a_j \leq a_m\}$;

Activity duration models $M\{\mu_i, \sigma_i^2\}$;

Resource peers $R\{R_i, ES (R_i), Cost (R_i) \mid i = 1,2,...K\}$

Output: Rescheduled task-resource list

// Stage 1: Optimising the makespan and cost for the integrated task-resource list through one metaheuristic algorithm

1)   *INITILISATION*();

// Running of metaheuristic rescheduling algorithms to minimise both makespan and cost of the integrated task-resource list

2) While (stopping condition is not met)

{

3)   *Run(Metaheuristic)*;

}

// return the best-so-far solution and record into the *SolutionSet*

4)   *Return(Solution, SolutionSet)*;

}

// Stage 2: Searching for the *BestSolution* from *SolutionSet*

5) While (not end of the *SolutionSet*)

{

// compare the compensation time of each *Solution* with the time deficit, discard the *Solution* if it is smaller than the time deficit

6)   *COMPARE (Solution.ct, TD(a_p))*;

// compare all remained *Solution* and set *BestSolution* as the one with the minimun cost

7)   *BestSolution = Min(Solution.cost)*;

}

8) Return the *BestSolution*;

// return the rescheduled integrated task-resource list and deploy

9)   *Deploy(L)*;

Figure 9.1 Two-stage local workflow rescheduling strategy.

candidates at each local step for the optimisation objective. However, the generated solution is not necessarily the best solution for the optimisation objective in an overall sense.

2. From the viewpoint of metaheuristics-based scheduling algorithms, the process of heuristics-based scheduling algorithms is to construct valid solutions. Since metaheuristics-based scheduling algorithms can use the valid solutions generated by heuristic scheduling algorithms as the initial input solution, the optimisation capability of metaheuristics-based scheduling algorithm is theoretically guaranteed to be better than that of heuristic scheduling algorithms.

To address the above two challenges, a novel general two-stage workflow local rescheduling strategy is designed for handing temporal violations. The pseudo-code for the general strategy is presented in Figure 9.1.

Here, 'two-stage' means a two-stage searching process to strike a balance between the handling of temporal violations and the on-time completion of other workflow instances, while 'local' means the rescheduling of 'local' workflow segments with existing resources. To handle temporal violations, the key optimisation objective is to maximise the compensation time, i.e. the difference of the scheduled execution time before and after rescheduling, in order to decrease the time deficit.

After rescheduling, the activities for the violated workflow instance will be allocated with resources of higher performance and/or given earlier time slots in the job queue for execution. However, if we only focus on the violated workflow instance, the execution time of other workflow instances could be delayed and may violate temporal constraints of their own, if any. Therefore, a balance between the handling of temporal violations and the on-time completion of other workflow instances needs to be considered in scientific workflow systems. Otherwise, the overall temporal QoS of scientific workflow systems will be potentially deteriorated.

As for local rescheduling, the first task is to identify the suitable size of the Task-Resource list. Our strategy utilises only existing local resources which are currently deployed in the system instead of recruiting additional resources outside the system. Meanwhile, unlike global rescheduling, which modifies the global Task-Resource list for the entire workflow instance, we focus only on the local workflow segment and optimise the integrated Task-Resource list. Here, the local workflow segment is defined as the set of workflow activities between the next activity of a necessary and sufficient checkpoint (the activity point where a temporal violation occurs) [23] and the end activity of the next local temporal constraint. As depicted in Figure 9.2, the integrated Task-Resource list is an integrated collection of local resources and the integrated DAG (Directed Acyclic Graph) task graph which defines the precedence relationships of all the activities in the local workflow segment and their co-allocated activities. Here, co-allocated activities are those which have been allocated to the same resources.

For example, in Figure 9.2, the local workflow segment contains activities a_{p+1} to a_{p+7}, and they are allocated to four different resources R_1 to R_4. Each resource maintains a local Task-List by its own scheduler given its input job queue. When temporal violation handling is triggered, the workflow management system will acquire the current Task-List of R_1 to R_4 and can automatically combine them into an integrated DAG task graph which consists of all the tasks — for instance, a total of n tasks — by assigning a pseudo start activity a_{Start} and pseudo end activity a_{End}. Therefore, an integrated Task-Resource list $L\{(a_i, R_j)|i = p + 1, \ldots, p + n, j = 1, 2, 3, 4\}$ is built and ready to be optimised.

As shown in Figure 9.1, the strategy has five major input parameters: the time deficit detected at the checkpoint, the integrated Task-Resource list, the DAG task graphs which define the precedence relationships between tasks, the normal distribution models for activity durations, and resources with their execution speed and the cost per time unit. Some additional information or parameters may also be required for each individual metaheuristic rescheduling algorithm. The first stage is to optimise the overall makespan and cost for the integrated Task-Resource list through any metaheuristics-based scheduling algorithm such as GA (detailed in Section 9.3.2) and ACO (detailed in Section 9.3.3). The first step is algorithm initialisation (Line 1) where different metaheuristic algorithms have their own initialisation process, such as chromosome coding for GA and setting of initial pheromones for ACO. After initialisation, the metaheuristic algorithms are executed until the predefined stopping condition, such as the maximum iteration times, is met (Line 2 to Line 3). During the metaheuristic algorithms-based optimisation process,

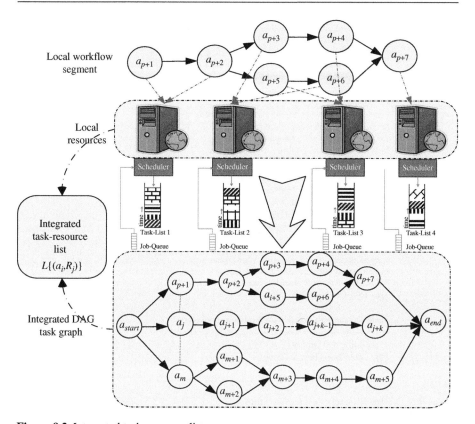

Figure 9.2 Integrated task-resource list.

a best-so-far solution can be produced in each iteration and recorded in the solution set. The second stage is to search for the best solution from the solution set (Line 5 to Line 7). During this searching stage, the occurred time deficit is first compared with the compensation time of each solution in the solution set (Line 6). Those solutions whose compensation time is smaller than the time deficit are discarded since they cannot handle the current temporal violation. Here, the compensation time is defined as the difference between the average makespan before rescheduling and the one after rescheduling. For those remained solutions, the one with the minimum cost is returned as the best solution (Line 7 to Line 8). Finally, according to the best solution, the integrated Task-Resource list is rescheduled and deployed on related resources (Line 9).

9.3.2   Metaheuristic Algorithm 1: GA

GA is a search technique often employed to find the exact or approximate solutions to optimisation and search problems [47,104]. GA is a specific class of

Genetic Algorithm

Input: Integrated Task-to-VM list $L\{(T_i,VM_j) \mid i = 1,2,..,n; j = 1,2,..,m\}$;
            Tasks $\{(T_i,Cost_i,Time_i,DAG) \{T_i > T_{i+1}\}\}$;
            Virtual Machines $\{VM_j, Price_j, Speed_j\}$.
Output: Optimised Scheduling Plan

//two dimensional encoding
1)   *Encoding(L)*;
// package-based random generation of initial populaton
2) Create initial *Population* of fixed size;
// **Optimising the overall makespan and cost**
3) While (stopping condition is not met)
     {
     //selecting *Parents* from *Population*
4)   *Selection (Population)*;
5)   *Crossover (Parents)* → *Children*;
     //change resource peer of a random cell
6)   *Mutation (Children)*;
     //validate with DAG, retain or discard
7)   *Validation (Children)*;
     //replace children of the worst fitness with the best one
8)   *Replace (WorstChild, BestChild)*;
     //check with the QoS constraints, retain or discard
9)   *Check (Children)*;
     }
// **Selecting the** *BestSolution* **according to user preferences**
10)   *BestSolution = Compare(SolutionSet,UserPref)*;
// decoding and deploy
11)   *Decoding(Best Solution)*;
12)   *Deploy(L)*.

Figure 9.3 GA-based rescheduling algorithm.

evolutionary algorithms inspired by evolutionary biology. In GA, every solution is represented with a string, also known as a chromosome, which follows the semantics defined by the encoding method. After encoding, the candidate solutions, i.e. the initial population, need to be generated as the basic search space. Within each generation, three basic GA operations, i.e. selection, crossover and mutation, are conducted to imitate the process of evolution in nature. Finally, after the stopping condition is met, the chromosome with the best fitness value is returned, representing the best solution found in the search space. That ends the whole GA process. In recent years, GA has been adopted to address large complex scheduling problems and proved to be effective in many distributed and dynamic resource environments, such as parallel processor systems and grid workflow systems [71,95].

The detailed introduction for each operation of GA can be found in our work in Refs [67] and [99] and hence omitted here. As depicted in Figure 9.3, the first searching phase of GA-based task-level scheduling is to optimise the overall makespan and cost for the integrated Task-Resource list through GA (Line 1 to Line 9). The GA algorithm starts from encoding (Line 1). Here a two-dimension encoding method is adopted. The first dimension represents the scheduled acts and the second represents the resource allocated to the corresponding act in the first dimension. GA starts with the generation of a fixed size initial population (Line 2). Because the quality of initial population is critical for the final outcome, a package-based random algorithm is applied to generate the initial population. After that, the algorithm starts searching for the best solution iteratively until the stopping condition, for example, the maximum generation, is met (Line 3 to Line 9). Three fundamental operations of GA including selection, crossover and mutation take actions in sequence. Stochastic universal sampling (SUS) [47] for selecting potentially useful solutions as parents for recombination is used in the selection operation (Line 4). SUS uses a single random value to sample all of the solutions by choosing them at evenly spaced intervals. The solution candidates generated during initialisation phase are all legal (i.e. they all satisfy the precedence relationship as defined in DAGs); however, conventional crossover will probably make some individuals illegal. To keep the diversity of the population, a single-point crossover strategy is employed (Line 5). When two parents are both legal, a single-point crossover ensures their children are legal. So before the mutation, the whole population is valid [75]. The third genetic operation is mutation (Line 6) where the allocated resource is mutated, i.e. substituted for another resource, at a randomly selected cell of a chromosome. The mutation rate is normally set to a small probability value such as 10% since mutation can easily destroy the correct precedence relationship and result in invalid solutions. The major effect of mutation is that it can introduce diversity into the population to help it jump out of local optimal traps. However, it can make some individuals invalid. These invalid individuals should be eliminated through validation and replacement (Line 7 and Line 8). Since a cloud workflow system is a market-oriented system, the candidate scheduling solution is expected to satisfy the QoS constraints according to the service contract. The last operation of the first phase is check which verifies whether the candidate individual should be retained or discarded.

During the second searching phase, the *SolutionSet* is compared with the user preference, i.e. *UserPref*, and the best scheduling plan L is deployed (Line 10 to Line 12). Both makespan and costs are taken into account in *UserPref*, which defines the specific preference of users towards the two factors. For example, the *UserPref* can be the minimum makespan, the minimum cost or a balance ratio between makespan and cost. The best scheduling plan (*BestSolution*) is selected from the satisfied population (Line 10). *BestSolution* is defined as the best solution according to *UserPref* among all the valid solutions. Since *BestSolution* is represented in the two dimensional vector, it should be decoded back to L as an integrated Task-to-VM list (Line 11). The last step of the whole algorithm is to deploy the L (Line12).

9.3.3 Metaheuristic Algorithm 2: ACO

In recent years, ACO, a type of optimisation algorithm inspired by the foraging behaviour of real ants in the wild has been adopted to address large complex scheduling problems and has proven to be quite effective in many distributed and dynamic resource environments, such as parallel processor systems and grid workflow systems [13,26].

The detailed introduction for each operation of ACO can be found in our work in Refs [99] and [60] and hence omitted here. As shown in Figure 9.4, the first

Ant Colony Optimisation

Input: Integrated Task-to-VM list $L\{(T_i,VM_j) \mid i = 1,2,...,n; j = ;1,2,...,m\}$;
             Tasks $\{T_i,Cost_i,Time_i,DAG\{T_i > T_{i+1}\}\}$;
             Virtual Machines $\{VM_j, Price_j, Speed_j\}$.

Output: Optimised Scheduling Plan

//**Optimising the overall makespan and cost**
//Initialisation of pheromone and other parameters for ACO algorithm
// package-based random generation
1) *INITIALISATION(ACO)*;
2) **While** (stopping condition is not met)
    {
// initialise each ant
      for each ant
      {
// select heuristics from duration-greedy, cost-greedy and overall-greedy
3)   *SELECTION(Heuristics)*;
// build tackling sequence TS based on the input DAG task graphs
4)   *BUILDING(TS, DAGs)*;
      }
// construct solutions
5)   **While** (not end of TS)
     {
// choose the resource for the next activity based on its earliest start time,
earliest end time, and the bias of B_{ij} (mapping resource R_j to activity a_i)
6)   *CHOOSE($a_i,a_i.est,eet,R\{R_j\},B_{ij}$)*;
// update the est and eet for all the subsequent activities;
7)   *UPDATE (est,eet)*;
// update local pheromone for both duration and cost
8)   *LOCALUPDATE($d\tau_{ij},c\tau_{ij}$)*;
     }
// update the global pheromone based on the makespan and cost of the best-
so-far solution
9)   *GLOBALUPDATE($d\tau_{ij},d\tau_{ij},makespan^{bs},cos\ t^{bs}$)*;
// return the best-so-far solution and record into the *SolutionSet*
10)   *RETURN(Solution, SolutionSet)*;
     }
// **Selecting the *BestSolution* according to user preferences**
11)   *BestSolution = COMPARE(SolutionSet,UserPref)*;
// deploy the scheduling plan
12)   *Deploy(L)*.

Figure 9.4 ACO-based rescheduling algorithm.

searching stage is to optimise the overall execution time and cost for the integrated Task-Resource list through ACO (Line 1 to Line 10). The ACO algorithm starts from initialisation of pheromone and all parameters (Line 1). In Ref. [27], two types of pheromone, namely $d\tau_{ij}$ and $c\tau_{ij}$, are defined. Here, $d\tau_{ij}$ denotes the desirability of mapping task a_i to resource R_j from the perspective of execution time while $c\tau_{ij}$ denotes the desirability from the perspective of execution cost. Afterwards, the ACO-based searching process iterates until the stopping condition, i.e. the maximum iteration times, is satisfied. During each iteration, a group of ants need to be initialised first (Line 3 to Line 4). Each ant starts by selecting one of the heuristics from duration-greedy, cost-greedy or overall-greedy which has specific preference on searching (Line 3). Then, the tackling sequence which arranges the order of tasks is built based on the input DAG task graph (Line 4).

During the solution construction process (Line 5 to Line 8), each activity is allocated to a specific resource according to its bias B_{ij} which is based on the value of pheromones and the heuristic information (Line 6). Meanwhile, after a specific choice of resources, the earliest start time *est* of the current activity is compared with the earliest end time *eet* of its predecessors to determine whether the current schedule can satisfy the precedence relationships defined in the DAG task graph. After a successful resource allocation, the *est* and *eet* for its subsequent activities are updated (Line 7). Here, a local updating process is conducted to decrease the local pheromone of $d\tau_{ij}$ and $c\tau_{ij}$ so that the following ant can have a higher probability of choosing other resources (Line 8). Evidently, the purpose of local updating is to enhance the diversity of the ACO algorithm. In contrast, after all ants have built their individual solutions, a global updating process is conducted to increase the pheromone along the path for the best-so-far solution so that the subsequent ants have higher probability to choose the same scheduling plan (Line 9). Therefore, the purpose of global updating is to reinforce the best-so-far solution in order to speed up the convergence of the ACO algorithm. Finally, at the end of iteration, the best-so-far solution is returned and added into the *SolutionSet* which serves as the input for the second searching stage (Line 10).

In the second searching stage, the *BestSolution* is retrieved from the *SolutionSet* (Line 11 to Line 12). The process is the same as the one described in GA. The *BestSolution* is selected according to the user preference *UserPref* (Line 11) and then the corresponding integrated Task-to-VM list is deployed.

9.3.4 Other Representative Metaheuristic Algorithms

Besides GA and ACO introduced above, other representative metaheuristic algorithms often used in workflow scheduling/rescheduling include PSO (Particle Swarm Optimisation) [107], GRASP (Greedy Randomised Adaptive Search Procedure) [105] and SA [6]. In this book, we do not intend to investigate all of the metaheuristics algorithms. Readers interested in an overview of representative metaheuristics-based algorithms may refer to [7]. Meanwhile, we have done some simulation experiments to evaluate and compare the performance of GA, ACO and the other three metaheuristics algorithms mentioned above. For detailed results, please refer to our document online[1].

9.4 Three-Level Temporal Violation Handling Strategy

The above sections have presented an overview of temporal violation handling strategies. In this section, we present the temporal violation handling strategies

---

[1] http://www.ict.swin.edu.au/personal/xliu/doc/HandlingFramework.rar

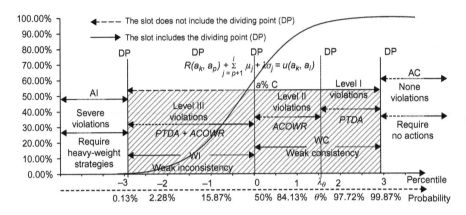

Figure 9.5 Fine-grained temporal violations based on three temporal violation handling strategies.

designed in our temporal framework in detail. As introduced in Section 9.2, there are many temporal violation handling strategies available. To save the cost for handling temporal violations, different scientific cloud workflow systems may choose a set of different temporal violation handling strategies to deal with different levels of temporal violations with small to large time deficits. In our temporal framework, as shown in Figure 9.5, three levels of fine-grained recoverable temporal violations including level I, level II and level III are defined and their corresponding light-weight temporal violation handling strategies are *PTDA*, *ACOWR* and *PTDA + ACOWR*, respectively.

As discussed in Section 8.2.1, apart from AC and AI, all the probability temporal consistency states within the probability range of (0.13%, 99.87%) may produce temporal violations but statistically can be recovered by light-weight handling strategies. In our temporal framework, the recoverable probability range is further divided into three levels of fine-grained temporal violations.

As can be seen in Figure 9.5, the dividing points include the normal percentile of λ_θ and 0 which correspond to the probability consistency states of $\theta\%$ and 50%, respectively. Here, $\theta\%$ denotes the minimum acceptable initial temporal consistency state, and it is usually specified through the negotiation between users and service providers for setting temporal constraints [62]. In practice, $\theta\%$ is normally around or above 84.13%, i.e. $\mu + \sigma$, which denotes reasonable confidence for on-time completion. Therefore, if current temporal consistency state of $\alpha\%$ is larger than $\theta\%$, the QoS contract still holds but slightly away from absolute consistency — in other words, there are still chances for temporal violations. Therefore, those temporal violations with the probability consistency states larger than $\theta\%$ are defined as level I temporal violations. As for the second dividing point of 50%, the motivation is the same as in multi-state-based temporal consistency models where the dividing point for weak consistency and weak inconsistency is defined with mean durations [18], since when the probability consistency state is of 50%, the workflow process needs to be completed within the sum of mean activity durations. Theoretically, in such a situation, the probabilities for temporal violation and non-violation for any distribution models are equally the same, i.e. 50%. Therefore, those temporal violations with probability consistency states equal to or larger than 50%, similar to conventional weak consistency states, are defined as level II temporal violations and a light-weight handling strategy is required to compensate the occurred time deficits and bring the current temporal consistency state back to at least $\theta\%$, i.e. the minimum acceptable temporal consistency state. As for those temporal violations with the probability consistency states smaller than 50%, similar to conventional weak inconsistency states, they are defined as level III temporal violations and more efforts compared with that of handling level II temporal violations are required to bring the current temporal consistency state back to at least $\theta\%$. However, since they are still within the recoverable probability range rather than absolute inconsistency, level III temporal violations can still be recovered by light-weight automatic handling strategies.

As discussed in Ref. [18], similar to *TDA*, the basic idea of *PTDA* is to automatically utilise the expected probability time redundancy of the subsequent workflow segments to compensate the current time deficits. *ACOWR*, as one type of workflow rescheduling strategies, tackles the violations of QoS constraints through optimising the current plan for Task-to-Resource assignment [60]. When temporal violations are detected, these strategies can be realised automatically without human interventions. Furthermore, *PTDA* produces only a small amount of calculations. *ACOWR*, as a type of metaheuristic searching algorithm, consumes more (yet acceptable) computing time but without recruiting additional resources. Therefore, as will also be verified through the simulation experiments demonstrated in Section 9.6, *PTDA*, *ACOWR* and the hybrid strategy of *PTDA* and *ACOWR* are effective candidates for handling temporal violations given the requirements of both *automation* and *cost-effectiveness* as presented in Section 9.1.2.

In the following, we present the algorithms for the three temporal violation handling strategies.

9.4.1   PTDA *for Level I Violations*

The basic idea of *PTDA* is the same as TDA presented in Section 9.2.1. However, since in this book, the time deficits are calculated based on our probability-based temporal consistency model and hence to differentiate our strategy from the conventional TDA strategy, it is named *PTDA*. The pseudo-code for *PTDA* is presented in Figure 9.6.

The actual process of *PTDA* is to borrow the expected time redundancy of the next workflow segment to compensate the current time deficit and then allocate the time deficit to the subsequent activities. The first task of *PTDA* is to calculate the expected time redundancy of the next workflow segment (Line 1). Normally, the next workflow segment is chosen as the workflow segment between the next activity of the checkpoint a_p, i.e. a_{p+1}, and the end activity of the next local temporal constraint, say a_{p+m} here. The expected time redundancy is defined as the

---

Strategy I: Probability Time Deficit Allocation

Input: Time deficit detected at activity a_p $TD(a_p)$;
         Next workflow segment WS $(a_{p+1}, a_{p+1},...a_{p+m})$;
         Temporal constraint $U(a_{p+1}, a_{p+m})$;
         Activity duration models $M\{\mu_i, \sigma_i^2\}$;
Output: Re-assigned temporal constraints for each activity $U\{U'(a_i) \mid i = p + 1,...p + m\}$;

// Calculating the expected time redundancy TR

1   $TR(a_{p+1}, a_{p+m}) = U(a_{p+1}, a_{p+m}) - \sum_{i=p+1}^{p+m}(\mu_i + \lambda_\theta * \sigma_i)$;

// allocating the time deficit to the subsequent activities based on their mean activity time redundancy

2)   for $i = p + 1$ to $p + m$

3) $U'(a_i) = U(a_i) - TR(a_{p+1}, a_{p+m}) * \dfrac{D(a_i) - M(a_i)}{\sum_{i=p+1}^{p+m}(D(a_i) - M(a_i))}$

            $= U(a_i) - TR(a_{p+1}, a_{p+m}) * \dfrac{\sigma_i}{\sum_{i=p+1}^{p+m}(\sigma_i)}$

// based on 3σ rule, $D(a_i) = \mu_i + 3\sigma_i$ and $M(a_i) = \mu_i$

4)   end for

5)   return $U\{U'(a_i) \mid i = p + 1,...p + m\}$

Figure 9.6 *PTDA* algorithm.

difference between the temporal constraint and the execution time for the minimum acceptable temporal consistency state (Line 1). The expected time redundancy can be borrowed to compensate the time deficits for level I temporal violations. After that, the expected time redundancy is allocated to the subsequent activities within the workflow segment according to the proportion of their mean activity time redundancy as defined in Ref. [18] (Line 2 to Line 4). After that, re-assigned temporal constraints for each activity are returned (Line 5). Therefore, the actual compensation process for *PTDA* is to tighten the temporal constraints of the subsequent activities so as to ensure that the current scientific workflow execution is close to absolute consistency. However, since *PTDA* does not decrease the actual activity durations of the subsequent activities, it can handle level I violations of some local workflow segments but has no effectiveness on global constraints, for example, the final deadline. To actually decrease the execution time of workflow segments (required by level II and level III temporal violations), more sophisticated handling strategies such as workflow rescheduling are required.

9.4.2 ACOWR *for Level II Violations*

Since the pseudo-code for *ACOWR* is the integrated pseudo-code of the two-stage local workflow rescheduling and ACO strategy, presented in Section 9.3.1 (Figure 9.1) and Section 9.3.3 (Figure 9.4), respectively, it is omitted here.

9.4.3 PTDA + ACOWR *for Level III Violations*

The hybrid strategy of *PTDA* and *ACOWR* (denoted as *PTDA + ACOWR*) is responsible for handling level III temporal violations. *ACOWR* is capable of removing most time deficits and handle level II temporal violations. However, due to the larger

Strategy III: PTDA+ACOWR

Input: Time deficit detected at activity a_p, $TD(a_p)$;

The next workflow segment WS $(a_{p+1}, a_{p+1}, ... a_{p+m})$;

Integrated task-resource list $L\{(a_i, R_j) | i = p+1, ... p+n, j = 1,2, ... K\}$;

DAG task graphs $DAG\{G_i | a_j \leq a_m\}$;

The temporal constraint $U(a_{p+1}, a_{p+n})$;

Activity duration models $M\{\mu_i, \sigma_i^2\}$;

Resource peers $R\{R_i, ES(R_i), Cost(R_i) | i = 1,2, ... K\}$.

Output: Rescheduled task-resource list

// **Stage 1: Try to adjust level III temporal violation back to level II by TDA**
// decrease the current time deficit by the expected time redundancy of the next
workflow segment but without allocating the time deficit

1) $TR(a_{p+1}, a_{p+n}) = U(a_{p+1}, a_{p+n}) - \sum\limits_{i=p+1}^{p+n}(\mu_i + \lambda_\theta * \sigma_i)$;

2) $TD(a_p) = TD(a_p) - TR(a_{p+1}, a_{p+m})$;

// **Stage 2: Compensate the remaining time deficit by ACOWR**

3) While $(TD(a_p) > 0$ or the stopping condition is not met)

{

// call Strategy II

4)   ACOWR();

// decrease the time deficit by the compensation time of the *BestSolution*

5) $TD(a_p) = TD(a_p) - BestSolution.ct$;

6)   if $TD(a_p) > 0$

// read in the second next workflow segment

{

7) $WS = WS(a_{p+m+1}, a_{p+m+2} ... a_{p+m+m'})$;

// update all the required information

8) $UPDATE(L\{\}, DAG\{\}, M\{\}, R\{\})$;

}

}

// return the rescheduled integrated task-resource list and deploy

9) DEPLOY(L)

Figure 9.7 *PTDA + ACOWR* algorithm.

amount of time deficits occurring in level III temporal violations, we present the hybrid strategy of *PTDA* and *ACOWR* to achieve stronger temporal violation handling capability. The pseudo-code for *PTDA + ACOWR* is presented in Figure 9.7.

The hybrid strategy starts with the first stage of *PTDA* (Line 1 to Line 2). However, here we utilise only the expected time redundancy to decrease the current time deficits without allocating them since the subsequent activities will be further rescheduled by *ACOWR*. The second stage is an iterative process of *ACOWR* (Line 3 to Line 8). Here, *ACOWR* is called for the first time to compensate the time deficit with the best solution for the subsequent workflow segment (Line 4 to Line 5). However, if the time deficit is not removed, the second subsequent workflow segment is read in to increase the size of local workflow segment and the input information is updated accordingly (Line 7 to Line 8). Afterwards, as the iteration process carries on, *ACOWR* will optimise additional workflow segments until the time deficit is entirely removed. In practice, according to our experimental results as will be demonstrated in Section 9.6, two consecutive workflow segments are usually more than enough to compensate the occurred time deficits for recoverable temporal violations. Therefore, *ACOWR* will normally be applied no more than twice in the *PTDA + ACOWR* strategy for handling level III temporal violations. Finally, the optimised integrated Task-Resource list will be returned and deployed (Line 9).

9.5 Comparison of GA- and ACO-based Workflow Rescheduling Strategies

9.5.1 Experimental Settings

In this section, comprehensive simulation and comparison experiments are conducted to evaluate GA- and ACO-based workflow rescheduling strategies from four important perspectives, including the optimisation rates for the makespan, the optimisation rates for the cost, the time-deficit compensation rates and the CPU time of itself. All the programme code as well as the experimental results can be found online[2].

Settings for Workflows

The basic experiment settings are presented in Table 9.1. Similar to the one shown in Figure 9.2, workflow processes in the integrated Task-Resource list are randomly generated as DAG task graphs with a random size of 3−5 activities. The mean duration of each task is randomly selected from 30 to 3,000 basic time units and its standard deviation is defined as 33% of its mean (a large standard deviation for valid normal distribution models where the samples are all positive numbers according to the '3σ' rule) to represent the highly dynamic performance of underlying resources. Each resource contains three attributes including resource ID, the execution speed and the execution cost. Here, the execution speed is defined as an integer from 1 to 5 where the execution time is equal to the mean duration divided by the execution speed. In each of the 10 experiment scenarios, half of the resources are with the speed of 1 and the others are with a random speed from 1 to 5. To simplify the setting, the price of each resource (for every 60 basic time units) in our experiment is defined as the execution speed plus a random number ranging from 1 to 3. For example, if a task is allocated to a resource with the execution speed of 2, then 2 basic units plus additional random 1−3 basic units, for example, 4 basic cost units, will be charged for every 60 basic time units consumed on such a resource (namely the price of the resource is 4).

As for the integrated Task-Resource list, it is defined with three attributes, being A (the number of total activities), W (the number of workflow instances) and R (the number of resources). Specifically, the number of total activities ranges from 50 to 300 including both workflow and non-workflow activities. The number of workflow segments increase accordingly from 5 to 50. The number of resources is constrained in a range of 3−20 since high-performance resources in scientific workflow systems usually maintain long job queues. QoS constraints including time constraint and cost constraint for each task are defined where time constraint is defined as the mean duration plus $1.28*\sqrt{variance}$ and cost constraint is defined as the triple of the corresponding time constraint. The makespan of a workflow is defined as the latest finished time on all the VMs and the total cost of a workflow is defined as the

---

[2] http://www.ict.swin.edu.au/personal/xliu/doc/HandlingFramework.rar

Table 9.1 Experimental Settings

Setting for Input Parameters

Workflow process setting	Randomly generated DAG task graphs with a random size of (3–5) activities for each local workflow segment
Duration distribution setting	Duration distribution of a_j is $N(u_j, \sigma_j^2)$ where $\mu_j = random(30,3000)$ and $\sigma_j = 33.3\% * \mu_j$
Resource setting	$R(R_i, ES(R_i), COST(R_i))$, resource R_i with the execution speed of $ES(R_i) = random(1,5)$ where the mean duration of a_j on resource R_i is $\mu_j / ES(R_i)$, and the resource price is $COST(R_i) = ES(R_i) + random(1,3)$
Time deficits setting	The time deficits are randomly set as 50–90% of the mean durations of the local workflow segments
Integrated task-resource list setting	$L(a_i, R_j)$ is defined with A (the number of activities), W (the number of workflow instances) and R (the number of local resources)

Setting for A, W and R

Round	A	W	R	Round	A	W	R
1	50	6	3	6	200	28	12
2	80	10	5	7	220	30	15
3	120	15	6	8	250	35	16
4	250	20	8	9	280	40	18
5	180	25	10	10	300	50	20

sum of task durations multiplied by the prices of their allocated VMs. As for the three basic performance measurements, the optimisation rate on makespan equals the mean makespan minus the minimum makespan, then divided by the mean makespan; the optimisation rate on cost equals to the mean cost minus the minimum cost, then divided by the mean cost; the CPU time used is defined as the average execution time of each algorithm running on a standard SwinDeW-C node.

Parameter Settings for GA

In GA, 50 new individuals are created during each iteration. The crossover rate is set to 0.7 and the mutation rate is 0.1. To make a trade-off between effectiveness and efficiency, we design a compound stopping condition with four parameters: the minimum iteration times, the maximum iteration times, the minimum increase of optimisation rate on time (the increase of optimisation rate on time: the minimum makespan of last iteration minus the minimum makespan of the current iteration and divided by that of the last iteration) and the minimum increase of optimisation rate on cost (similar to that of makespan). Specifically, the evolutionary process iterates at least a minimum of 100 times. After 100 iterations, the iteration will stop on condition that the maximum iteration times are met, the increase of the optimisation rate on time is less than 0.02, or the increase of optimisation rate on cost is less than 0.02.

Parameter Settings for ACO

In ACO, 50 new ants are created in each iteration. Since we focus on both the reduction of makespan and the reduction of cost, half of them are created as duration-greedy and another half as cost-greedy. The maximum iteration times are set as 1,000 and the minimum iteration times are 100. The weights of pheromone and heuristic information are set to be 1 and 2. The probability of selecting the implementation with the largest value of B_{ij} is 0.8. The local pheromone updating rate is 0.1 and the global pheromone updating rate is also 0.1. For fairness, the stopping condition is the same as defined in GA.

Definition for Fitness Value

Fitness value is the fundamental measurement for a candidate solution. In our strategy, we seek balanced scheduling plans where total makespan and total cost can be optimised in an unbiased fashion. Therefore, in both GA and ACO, the function for the fitness value is defined as follows:

$$FitnessValue(TotalMakespan, TotalCost) = (TotalMakespan + 3 \times TotalCost)^{-1}$$

where *TotalMakespan* and *TotalCost* are the total makespan and total cost of a candidate solution, respectively.

Here, the fitness value is defined as a reciprocal relation to the sum of total makespan and total cost since the smaller the sum, the better the solution, i.e. its fitness value. Meanwhile, note that the *TotalCost* is multiplied by a factor of 3. Since the basic time unit and the basic cost unit are usually different in the real world. For example, in a scientific workflow system, if the basic time unit is one second and the basic cost unit is one dollar, the value of total makespan is normally much higher than that of total cost. For instance, for the use of Amazon EC2 standard on-demand instances service (http://aws.amazon.com/ec2/pricing/), the default price is $0.12 per instance hour (i.e. 3,600 seconds).

Therefore, in order to adjust the makespan and the cost to the same order of magnitude, a factor is usually needed to multiple the value of cost. This factor can be selected through empirical study of the historical data or through simulation experiments. In this chapter, according to our experimental settings presented in Table 9.1, we have tried different candidates for the factor such as 2, 3, 5, 8, 10 and 15. Based on the experimental results, we find out that 3 is one of the best candidates that can adjust the makespan and the cost to the same order of magnitude for most cases. Therefore, we use 3 as the factor in the function for the fitness value as defined above.

9.5.2 Experimental Results

To evaluate and compare the performance of our GA- and ACO-based rescheduling strategy, four measurements are investigated: the optimisation ratio on total makespan, the optimisation ratio on total cost, the compensation ratio on violated workflow segment and the CPU time.

Specifically, the optimisation ratio on total makespan is defined as follows:

$$OptMakespan = 100\% - \frac{AfterTotalMakespan}{BeforeTotalMakespan}$$

where *AfterTotalMakespan* is the total makespan, i.e. the completion time, of the entire activity set in the integrated Task-Resource list, after workflow rescheduling; and *BeforeTotalMakespan* is the total makespan before workflow rescheduling. Here, in each round of experiment, for purposes of comparison, the average total makespan of all the best candidates in each generation of the GA-based rescheduling strategy is specified as the value for *BeforeTotalMakespan*.

The optimisation ratio on total cost is defined as follows:

$$OptCost = 100\% - \frac{AfterTotalCost}{BeforeTotalCost}$$

where *AfterTotalCost* is the total cost, i.e. the running cost, of the entire activity set in the integrated Task-Resource list, after workflow rescheduling; and *BeforeTotalCost* is the total running cost before workflow rescheduling. Similar to the total makespan, for the comparison purpose, the average total cost of all the best candidates in each generation of the GA-based rescheduling strategy is specified as the value for *BeforeTotalCost*.

The compensation ratio is defined as follows:

$$CompentationRatio = 100\% - \frac{AfterLocalMakespan}{BeforeLocalMakespan}$$

where *AfterLocalMakespan* is the execution time of the activities in the local work-flow segment of the violated workflow instance, after workflow rescheduling (with either GA or ACO); and *BeforeLocalMakespan* is the corresponding execution time before workflow rescheduling (with either GA or ACO). Please note that here, the average makespan before workflow rescheduling with GA is not used as the bench-mark. Since we want to investigate the capability of these strategies in the handling of temporal violations, we need to compare the local makespan of the violated workflow segment before and after the same rescheduling strategy in the same workflow instance.

The CPU time is defined as follows:

$$CPUTime = Start(Rescheudling) - End(Rescheduling)$$

where *Start (Rescheduling)* is the system time at the start of the rescheduling strat-egy; and *End (Rescheduling)* is the system time when the rescheduling strategy is successfully completed, i.e. a satisfactory regenerated scheduling plan is found and ready to be implemented.

Note that, in order to find a balanced solution with total makespan and cost, the best solution in our experiments is defined as the solution with the largest fitness value. Therefore, the best total makespan for each round of experiment is the total makespan of the solution with the best fitness value, and its cost is thus defined as the best total cost. The same rule is also applied to the best local makespan for cal-culating the compensation ratio.

In the rest of this section, for ease of presentation, we use ACO to stand for ACO-based rescheduling strategy and GA to stand for GA-based rescheduling strategy.

The results of optimisation ratio on makespan are presented in Figure 9.8. Figure 9.8A depicts the optimisation ratio on total makespan for the total 10 rounds of experiments. For ACO, the maximum, minimum and mean optimisation ratios for makespan are 29.0%, 10.0% and 15.9%, respectively. As for GA, the maxi-mum, minimum and mean optimisation ratios for makespan are 29.0%, 13.0% and 19.9%, respectively. The optimisation ratio for both GA and ACO is on a roughly decreasing trend with the growing number of activities (including both workflow activities and general tasks). In comparison, GA has a relatively more stable performance and a higher optimisation ratio than that of ACO.

Figure 9.8B depicts the best total makespan for each round of experiment mea-sured in basic time units, and the average total makespan for the candidates gener-ated by GA is also shown in the figure for the comparison purpose. It can be easily seen that the best total makespan for the candidates generated by GA and ACO in each round is not far from each other, and 6 out of the 10 rounds of experiments

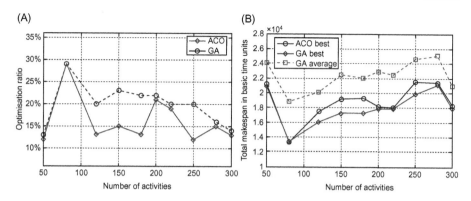

Figure 9.8 Optimisation on total makespan: (A) optimisation ratio on total makespan and (B) total makespan for each round of experiment.

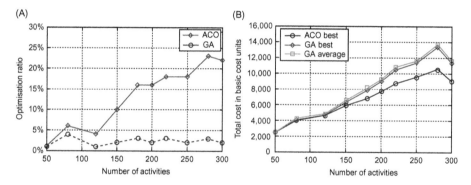

Figure 9.9 Optimisation on total cost: (A) optimisation ratio on total cost and (B) total cost for each round of experiment.

are very close. Note that due to different settings as in Table 9.1, the total makespan for each round is not simply on the rise with the growing number of activities since the number of resources also increases although not in a linear way.

The results of optimisation ratio on cost are presented in Figure 9.9. Figure 9.9A depicts the optimisation ratio on total cost for the total 10 rounds of experiments. For ACO, the maximum, minimum and mean optimisation ratios for cost are 23.0%, 1.0% and 13.4%, respectively. As for GA, the maximum, minimum and mean optimisation ratios for makespan are 4.0%, 1.0% and 2.3%, respectively. Unlike the optimisation ratio on makespan, the results of GA and ACO are very different where ACO significantly outperforms GA.

Figure 9.9B depicts the best total cost for each round of experiment measured in basic cost units, and the average total cost for the candidates generated by GA is also shown in the figure for the comparison purpose. It can be easily seen that the total cost for each round of experiment is increasing rapidly with the growing number of activities. However, there is a small decline at the last round. This is mainly because with the different settings for the activities and resources as in Table 9.1, the total cost for each round does not simply increase in a linear way. Meanwhile, the best total cost for the candidates generated by GA and ACO in each round is very close at the beginning, but the difference becomes larger when the number of activities grows.

The results of compensation on violated workflow segments are depicted in Figure 9.10. Figure 9.10A depicts the compensation ratio for each round of experiment. For ACO, the maximum, minimum and mean compensation ratios are 69.0%, 35.0% and 58.5%, respectively. As for GA, the maximum, minimum and mean compensation ratios are 68.0%, 35.0% and 55.5%, respectively. It is clear that the compensation ratios for GA and ACO are significantly close to each other, i.e. their handling capabilities on temporal violations are almost the same. The compensation ratio for both GA and ACO is on a roughly increasing trend with the growing number of activities.

Figure 9.10B presents the best local makespan for the violated workflow segment in each round of experiment, and the average local makespan is also presented for the comparison purpose. The best local makespan for the candidates generated by GA and ACO are very close to each other for all the cases. The results actually show that both GA and ACO can find the candidate solutions with the best local makespan for the violated workflow segment.

Figure 9.10C presents the optimisation ratio on total makespan with best local makespan. In our two-stage workflow local rescheduling strategy, the first stage is for the optimisation of total makespan and total cost (as the results shown in Figure 9.8 and Figure 9.9), and the second stage is for seeking the solution with the largest compensation ratio among the best candidate solutions found in the first searching stage. Since the final solution the system applied is the one with the best local makespan, we need to further investigate its performance on the total makespan, as the final solution is not necessarily the best solution found in the first searching stage.

As shown in Figure 9.10C, for ACO, the maximum, minimum and average optimisation ratios on total makespan with best local makespan are 30.0%, 12.0% and 17.9%, respectively. As shown in Figure 9.8A, the maximum, minimum and mean optimisation ratios for total makespan are 29.0%, 10.0% and 15.9%, respectively. It is interesting to see that the optimisation ratios on total makespan with best local makespan in the second searching stage are in general better than the optimisation ratios on total makespan in the first searching stage. The main reason is that the optimisation ratios on total makespan in the first stage are calculated based on the average total makespan of the best solutions found in each iteration, while the optimisation ratios on total makespan with best local makespan in the second stage are calculated based on the makespan of the final solution. Therefore, the results actually show that the final solution found by ACO is not only the one with the best local makespan but also the one with the total makespan better than the average of the best solutions found in each iteration in the first searching stage. GA has a similar performance: its maximum, minimum and average optimisation ratios on total makespan with best local makespan are 32.0%, 13.0% and 22.2%, respectively, while the

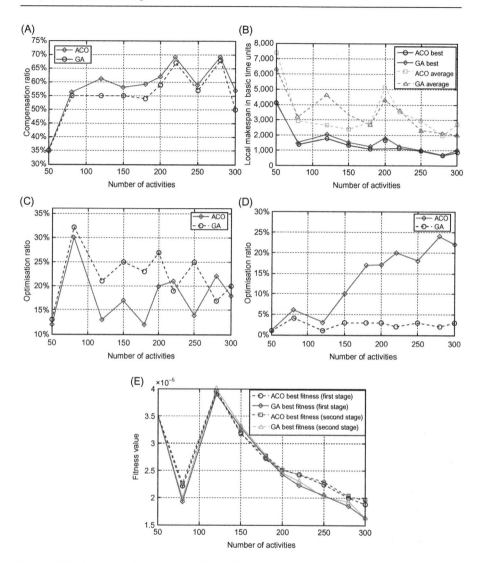

Figure 9.10 Compensation on violated workflow segment: (A) compensation ratio for each round of experiment; (B) local makespan for each round of experiment; (C) optimisation ratio on total makespan with best local makespan; (D) optimisation ratio on total cost with best local makespan and (E) best fitness value for each round of experiment.

maximum, minimum and mean optimisation ratios for the total makespan in the first stage are 29.0%, 13.0% and 19.9%, respectively. Moreover, by comparing Figure 9.10C and Figure 9.8A, we can easily see that the behaviours of the curves for GA and ACO in Figure 9.7C are very similar to their behaviours in Figure 9.8A.

Based on such a result, we can claim that our two-stage workflow local rescheduling strategy, with either GA or ACO, is capable of compensating the violated workflow segment (searching for the best local makespan) as well as optimising the total makespan of the entire integrated Task-Resource list (searching for the best total makespan).

For the similar reason, we also investigate the optimisation ratio on total cost with best local makespan as presented in Figure 9.10D. As shown in Figure 9.10D, for ACO, the maximum, minimum and average optimisation ratios for total cost with the best local makespan are 24.0%, 1.0% and 13.8%, respectively. As shown in Figure 9.7A, the maximum, minimum and mean optimisation ratios for total cost are 23.0%, 1.0% and 13.4%, respectively. As for GA, the maximum, minimum and average optimisation ratios on total makespan with best local makespan are 4.0%, 1.0% and 2.5%, respectively. While the maximum, minimum and mean optimisation ratios for makespan are 4.0%, 1.0% and 2.3%, respectively. The reason for such results can be explained similarly as above for the optimisation rations on makespan. Moreover, by comparing Figure 9.10D and Figure 9.9A, we can also see that the behaviours of the curves for GA and ACO in Figure 9.10D are very similar to their behaviours in Figure 9.9A. Based on such a result, we can claim that our two-stage workflow local rescheduling strategy, with either GA or ACO, is capable of compensating the violated workflow segment (searching for the best local makespan) as well as optimising the total cost of the entire integrated Task-Resource list (searching for the best total cost).

To give a more direct and clearer view, Figure 9.10E shows the best fitness value for the first searching stage and the second searching stage in each round of experiment. It can be easily seen that, for either GA or ACO, the best fitness values for the two searching stages are almost the same in each round of experiment. Meanwhile, the distances between the best fitness values of GA- and ACO-generated candidates in each round are very close to each other. However, in 6 out of 10 rounds, ACO performs slightly better than GA. Therefore, the results clearly show that our two-stage workflow local rescheduling strategy can find the candidates with best compensation rates in the second searching stage to handle temporal violations while maintaining similar fitness value to the best candidates found in the first searching stage for optimisation of total makespan and total cost.

The results of CPU time for both GA and ACO in each round of experiment are presented in Figure 9.11. For ACO, the maximum, minimum and mean CPU times are 9,540.5, 1,453.1 and 4,730.1 milliseconds, respectively. As for GA, the maximum, minimum and mean compensation ratios are 4,182.8, 2,368.9 and 3,257.6 milliseconds, respectively. It is clear that ACO requires much more CPU time than GA. The CPU time for ACO follows a steadily increasing trend with the growing of number of activities. GA also follows an increasing trend but in a much slower way. In an overall sense, the CPU time for both GA and ACO are all trivial compared with the execution time of scientific workflow activities which normally take minutes or hours.

To summarise, based on the results shown in Figure 9.8 and Figure 9.9, both GA and ACO can effectively optimise the total makespan and total cost of the entire integrated Task-Resource list. Furthermore, based on the results shown in Figure 9.10C and Figure 9.10D, we can claim that our two-stage workflow local rescheduling strategy is capable of compensating the violated workflow segment as

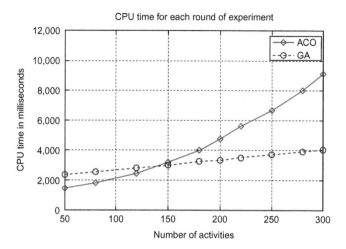

Figure 9.11 CPU time.

well as optimising the entire integrated Task-Resource list on both total makespan and total cost. Therefore, the requirements for rescheduling strategies for handling temporal violations as analysed in Section 9.1.2 are successfully met.

Strategy Ranking Based on User Preference

The comprehensive evaluation results have been demonstrated above for both the GA- and ACO-based rescheduling strategies to illustrate the effectiveness of our general two-stage workflow local rescheduling strategies. However, as for which strategy should be employed in the scientific workflow system to handle temporal violations, a ranking function is required to make a decision based on user preference. The four basic measurements (including the optimisation ratio on total makespan, the optimisation ratio on total cost, the compensation ratio on violated workflow segment and the CPU time of the scheduling strategy) are used here for evaluation and comparison. Therefore, the ranking function is also designed based on these four measurements. For fairness, the average performance on each measurement for both GA and ACO is presented in Table 9.2.

The ranking function is defined as follows:

$$Rank(OptMakespan, OptCost, CompRatio, CPUTime)$$

$$= w_1 \times \frac{OptMakespan}{\sum_{i=1}^{k} OptMakespan_i} + w_2 \times \frac{OptCost}{\sum_{i=1}^{k} OptCost_i} + w_3 \times \frac{CompRatio}{\sum_{i=1}^{k} CompRatio_i}$$

$$+ w_4 \times \frac{CPUTime}{\sum_{i=1}^{k} CPUTime_i}$$

Table 9.2 Comparison of Basic Measurements

Rescheduling Strategy	ACO	GA
Average OptMakespan	15.9%	19.9%
Average OptCost	13.4%	2.3%
Average CompRatio	58.5%	55.5%
Average CPUTime	4730.1 milliseconds	3257.6 milliseconds

Here, the weight sector $\{w_1, w_2, w_3, w_4\}$ can be defined according to user preference. In this chapter, since our focus is on handling temporal violations, the compensation ratio is set with the largest weight. For instance, we set the weight vector as {0.2, 0.2, 0.5, 0.1}. Then, according to the ranking function above, the rank values for GA and ACO are 0.575 and 0.425, respectively. Therefore, we select the ACO-based rescheduling strategy, i.e. *ACOWR*, as the temporal violation handling strategy in our SwinDeW-C scientific workflow system. Note that different weight vectors may result in the selection of different strategies, but since the average *CompRatio* of GA and ACO are very close, their handling capabilities are thus very similar.

9.6 Evaluation of Three-Level Temporal Violation Handling Strategy

The experimental results demonstrated in this section include two parts: (1) the comparison results of the violation rates of local and global temporal violations for our three-level temporal violation handling strategy, the standalone *PTDA* and the standalone *NIL* and (2) the comparison results of the violation handling cost for our three-level temporal violation handling strategy, the standalone *ACOWR* and the standalone *PTDA + ACOWR*.

9.6.1 Violation Rates of Local and Global Temporal Constraints

As introduced in Section 9.4, in our temporal framework, the three-level temporal violation handling strategy is applied correspondingly when any of the three levels of temporal violations are detected. As for standalone *PTDA* and *NIL*, they will deal with all temporal violations exactly the same. Note that since *NIL* takes no actions for temporal violations, the violations rates for *NIL* are actually equal to the natural violation rates given the execution of the simulated scientific cloud workflows. As can be seen in Figure 9.12A, the violation rate of local temporal constraints (local violation rate for short) behaves stably under different constraint settings. For example, the average local violation rate is around 15% in COM(1.00) where the probability for on-time completion is 84.1%. As for *PTDA*, it can reduce the local violation rates when the size of scientific workflow is small. However, it

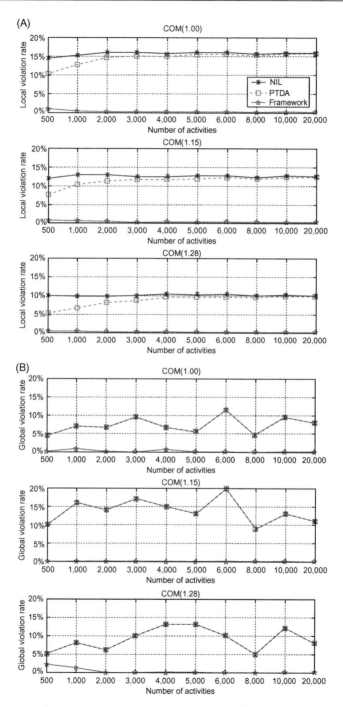

Figure 9.12 Handling of temporal violations: (A) local violation rate and (B) global violation rate.

behaves poorly when the number of activities exceeds 4,000. As analysed in Section 9.2.1, since *PTDA*, similar to TDA, does not compensate time deficits, it cannot postpone temporal violations any more when the time deficits accumulate to become large enough. With our three-level temporal violation handling strategy, the local violation rate is kept close to zero since the three handling strategies, *PTDA*, *ACOWR* and *PTDA + ACOWR*, can be applied dynamically to tackle different levels of temporal violations. The average local violation rates with our three-level temporal violation handling strategy in each round are 0.16%, 0.13% and 0.09%, respectively, i.e. an overall average of 0.127%.

Figure 9.12B shows the results on global violation rates. Since *PTDA* has no effect on global violations, the global violation rates for *NIL* and *PTDA* are overlapping. The global violation rates for *NIL* and *PTDA* behave very unstably but increase roughly with the number of activities while decreasing with the value of normal percentiles. The average global violation rates for *NIL* and *PTDA* in each round are 14.6%, 13.8% and 9.0%, respectively. With our temporal framework, the global violation rate is kept close to zero since most local temporal violations are handled automatically along workflow executions. The average global violation rates of our temporal framework in each round are 0.2%, 0.0% and 0.3%, respectively, i.e. an overall average of 0.167%.

In our three-level temporal violation handling strategy, *PTDA* is only responsible for level I violations and it is applied together with *ACOWR* for larger violations. Standalone *ACOWR* handles level II violations and its capability is defined according to its average *CompensationRatio* which is 58.5% given the experimental results shown in Figure 9.10. As for *PTDA + ACOWR* (where the maximum iteration times for *ACOWR* are set as 2), since the initial temporal consistency is around 90% and the average local violation rate for the three rounds of experiments are 0.13% (which is very close to 0%), the average *CompensationRatio* for *PTDA + ACOWR* should be around or over 90% so as to maintain a local violation rate near 0%.

9.6.2 Cost Analysis for a Three-Level Handling Strategy

We first take a look at the number of temporal violations (including all the three levels of temporal violations and non-recoverable temporal violation if any) in scientific workflows. Since our checkpoint selection strategy is necessary and sufficient, the results on the number of temporal violations are exactly the same as the number of checkpoints in scientific workflows as shown in Figure 7.2. The results have shown that the number of temporal violations increases accordingly with the growth of workflow size and the noises. Here, for ease of discussion without losing generality, we conduct the cost analysis based on the results on temporal violations for COM(1.28) without noises.

In our temporal framework, there are three temporal violation handling strategies including *PTDA*, *ACOWR* and *PTDA + ACOWR*. As can be seen in Figure 9.6, the computation cost of *PTDA* is negligible compared with that of *ACOWR*. In such a case, the cost of *PTDA + ACOWR* (including a maximum 2 times for

Table 9.3 Experimental Results on the Times of Temporal Violation Handling

Workflow Size	Total Times of Violation Handling	Total Times of *PTDA*	Total Times of *ACOWR*	Total Times of *PTDA* + *ACOWR*	Equivalent Times of *ACOWR*
Three-Level Handling Strategy					
2,000	43.8	4.3	33.7	5.8 (3.5(2), 2.3(1))	43.0
5,000	102.5	11.5	81.3	9.7 (6.2(2), 3.5(1))	97.2
10,000	195.8	23.5	157.2	15.1 (9.8(2), 5.3(1))	182.1
Standalone *ACOWR*					
2,000	49.5	NIL	49.5	NIL	49.5
5,000	123.8	NIL	123.8	NIL	123.8
10,000	248.6	NIL	248.6	NIL	248.6
Standalone *PTDA* + *ACOWR*					
2,000	46.3	NIL	NIL	46.3(4.1(2), 42.2(1))	50.4
5,000	118.5	NIL	NIL	118.5(12.2(2), 106.3(1))	130.7
10,000	239.2	NIL	NIL	239.2(21.5(2), 217.7(1))	260.7

ACOWR) can be regarded as either the same as or twice that of *ACOWR* depending on how many times that *ACOWR* is facilitated. Therefore, to ease our discussion, we can use the equivalent number of times for the application of *ACOWR* to represent the cost (and/or overhead) given that the average CPU time for running *ACOWR* once in a SwinDeW-G node is 4.73 seconds as indicated in Figure 9.7. Here, with various scientific workflows same as in Figure 9.12, we compare the cost of a standalone *ACOWR* and the cost of standalone *PTDA* + *ACOWR* with that of our temporal framework. Here, for purposes of comparison, the standalone *ACOWR* and standalone *PTDA* + *ACOWR* are implemented separately as the sole strategies for handling all three levels of temporal violations. The experiment settings are the same as in COM(1.28). Given similar global violation rates, the results for our temporal framework and the two standalone strategies are shown in Table 9.3.

As discussed above, the total cost for each strategy is calculated as the equivalent times for the application of *ACOWR*. As shown in Table 9.3, for our three-level handling strategy with 2,000 activities, on average, the total times of *PTDA* are 4.3 (for level I temporal violation), the total times of *ACOWR* (for level II temporal violation) are 33.7 and the total times of *PTDA* + *ACOWR* are 5.8 (for level III temporal violation and non-recoverable temporal violation if any) where 3.5 times with *ACOWR* twice and 2.3 with *ACOWR* once. Therefore, in such a case, the equivalent times of *ACOWR* are calculated as $33.7 + 3.5*2 + 2.3*1 = 43.0$. The other scenarios can be calculated in a similar way. Meanwhile, we can see that with 10,000 activities, for the total of 195.8 violations, the ratio of level I, level II and level III temporal violations (and non-recoverable temporal violation if any) are 12.0%, 80.3%, and 7.7%, respectively. The experimental results show that our three-level handling strategy has the smallest number of total temporal violation handling among all the strategies where the equivalent times of *ACOWR* for the workflow sizes of 2,000, 5,000 and 10,000 are 43.0, 97.2 and 182.1, respectively. This is mainly because in our temporal framework, different levels of temporal violations will be handled by their corresponding temporal violation handling strategies with the least cost. As for the standalone *ACOWR* and *PTDA + ACOWR*, their equivalent times of *ACOWR* are actually very close to each other. The main reason is that in the standalone *PTDA + ACOWR*, *ACOWR* will be executed either once or twice according to the level of the occurred temporal violations, for example, once for level I or level II, and maybe twice for level III. Therefore, the total cost of *PTDA + ACOWR*, i.e. the total times for the application of *ACOWR* in *PTDA + ACOWR*, is actually very close to that of the standalone *ACOWR*. For the standalone *PTDA + ACOWR*, for example, the cost reductions by our temporal framework are 14.7%, 25.6% and 30.1%, respectively, for the workflow size of 2,000, 5,000 and 10,000. Therefore, we can claim that our temporal framework is cost-effective. Comprehensive results including the results for other workflows can be found in our online document (see footnote 8).

Note that we have also investigated several expensive heavy-weight temporal violation handling strategies. Here, we take 'Adding a New Resource' ('Add' in short)[3] as an example; the time overhead for Add mainly consists of two parts, namely the data transfer time for workflow activities and the set-up time for a new resource. Given similar data transfer time in *ACOWR* and Add due to the re-mapping of tasks and resources, the set-up time for a new resource in our simulation environment is normally several minutes, similar to that of a reserved resource in the Amazon Elastic Compute Cloud (EC2, http://aws.amazon.com/ec2/). Therefore, the time overhead for Add is very large and thus not suitable for handling temporal violations. Furthermore, the monetary cost for reserving and using a new resource is much higher in comparison to the computation cost required for *ACOWR*. As for the other representative strategies such as Stop and Restart [30], Processor Swapping [30] and Workflow Restructure [88], they are either similar to Add or require human interventions. Therefore, given the basic requirements of *automation* and *cost-effectiveness* for handling recoverable temporal violations, all these expensive strategies are not suitable candidates. Detailed results have been included in our online document (see footnote 9).

---

[3] Here, a new resource is a hot online machine in the system. The set-up time for a cold offline machine will normally be much higher.

10 Conclusions and Contribution

The technical details for our novel probabilistic temporal framework have all been addressed in the previous chapters. In this chapter, we summarise the whole book. This chapter is organised as follows. Section 10.1 presents an overall cost analysis for the temporal framework. Section 10.2 summarises the contents of the whole book. Section 10.3 outlines the main contributions of this book. Finally, Section 10.4 points out the future work.

10.1 Overall Cost Analysis for Temporal Framework

This book presents a framework which can cost-effectively deliver high temporal QoS in scientific cloud workflow systems. As demonstrated in Section 9.6, based on our temporal framework, the average global violation rate of simulated scientific cloud workflows is 0.167%, and the average local violation rate is 0.13%. Therefore, we can claim that high temporal QoS in scientific cloud workflow systems can be achieved with the support of our temporal framework.

Based on the achievement of high temporal QoS, we further analyse whether our temporal framework achieves cost-effectiveness. The overall running cost of the temporal framework consists of the time overheads and monetary cost for each component. Specifically, our temporal framework consists of three major components, viz. Component I — temporal constraint setting, Component II — temporal consistency monitoring and Component III — temporal violation handling.

For Component I (temporal constraint setting), with the support of an accurate time-series-pattern-based forecasting strategy (presented in Chapter 5) and the four basic building blocks (presented in Section 6.3.1), high-quality coarse-grained temporal constraints can be assigned through an effective negotiation process between service users and service providers. Afterwards, fine-grained temporal constraints can be derived and propagated along scientific cloud workflows in an automatic fashion. Therefore, given a set of high-quality coarse-grained and fine-grained temporal constraints, the time overheads and computation cost for temporal constraints setting are much smaller compared with conventional manual settings. Therefore, we can claim that Component I is cost-effective.

For Component II (temporal consistency monitoring), presented in Chapter 7, with the novel probability-based temporal consistency model (presented in Section 6.2) and the definition of statistically recoverable and non-recoverable temporal violations (presented in Section 8.2.1), only one type of checkpoint needs to

Temporal QoS Management in Scientific Cloud Workflow Systems. DOI: 10.1016/B978-0-12-397010-7.00010-0

be selected and only one type of temporal consistency state needs to be verified. Therefore, given the same necessity and sufficiency, the overall cost for checkpoint selection and temporal verification can be significantly reduced compared with conventional multi-state-based temporal consistency-based strategies. Therefore, we can claim that Component II is cost-effective.

For Component III (temporal violation handling), with the novel adaptive temporal violation handling point selection strategy (presented in Chapter 8) which selects only a small subset of necessary and sufficient checkpoints, and the three-level temporal violation handling strategy (presented in Chapter 9) which consists of three light-weight handling strategies, viz. *PTDA* and *ACOWR* (based on the presented general two-stage local workflow rescheduling strategy) and *PTDA* + *ACOWR*, the overall cost for temporal violation handing can be significantly reduced while maintaining high temporal QoS compared with conventional temporal violation handling which is conducted at every necessary and sufficient checkpoint. Therefore, we can claim that Component III is cost-effective.

Note that the performance of the temporal framework may vary in different scientific cloud workflow system environments. Actually, in order to achieve the best performance, the settings and parameters for the components in our temporal framework can all be modified according to the real-world system environments. Therefore, based on the statistics of system logs or other sources of historical data in the real world, simulation experiments should be conducted first to specify the best parameters for these components in our framework instead of using default values.

To conclude, based on systematic analysis for the lifecycle support of temporal QoS in scientific cloud workflow systems, a series of new concepts, innovative strategies and algorithms have been designed to successfully fulfil the system requirements of each component in a cost-effective fashion. Therefore, we can claim that our probabilistic temporal framework can indeed achieve the cost-effective delivery of high QoS in scientific cloud workflow systems.

10.2   Summary of This Book

The research objective described in this book is to investigate a series of new concepts, innovative strategies and algorithms for a temporal framework in order to achieve cost-effective delivery of high temporal QoS in scientific cloud workflow systems. The book was organised as follows:

- Chapter 1 introduced temporal QoS in scientific cloud workflow systems. A motivating example in astrophysics has been demonstrated to analyse the problems for delivering high temporal QoS in scientific cloud workflow systems. Chapter 1 also described the aims of this work, the key issues to be addressed in this book and the structure of this book.
- Chapter 2 overviewed the general related work on temporal QoS in workflow systems and analysed their limitations. Specifically, a temporal consistency model is used to define temporal consistency states; temporal constraint setting is to assign both global and local temporal constraints at workflow build time; temporal checkpoint selection and

temporal verification are the main steps for the monitoring of workflow execution and the detection of temporal violations; temporal violation handling is to compensate the existing time deficits with temporal violation handling strategies.

- Chapter 3 demonstrated a prototype scientific cloud workflow system, SwinDeW-C with its cloud testing bed SwinCloud, which served as the simulation environment for the experiments demonstrated in this book.
- Chapter 4 presented the overview of our probabilistic framework. The basis of the framework is a novel probability-based temporal consistency model where fine-grained temporal consistency states can be quantitatively measured by probability confidence values. In order to facilitate the lifecycle support of high temporal QoS for cloud workflow applications, our framework is composed of three main components — temporal constraint setting, temporal consistency monitoring and temporal violation handling — which were further illustrated in three separate components.

  The main technical details of the framework were presented separately in three components, including Component I for temporal constraint setting (consisting of Chapters 5 and 6), Component II for temporal consistency monitoring (consisting of Chapter 7) and Component III for temporal violation handling (consisting of Chapters 8 and 9).
- Chapter 5 presented a statistical time-series-pattern-based forecasting strategy for cloud workflow activity duration intervals. Specifically, based on a novel time-series segmentation algorithm, statistical time-series patterns and their associated turning points can be discovered to facilitate the forecasting of activity duration intervals. Comparison experiments with representative forecasting strategies show the better accuracy of our forecasting strategy.
- Chapter 6 presented a novel probabilistic temporal constraint setting strategy. Based on the joint weighted normal distribution model, the execution times of the workflow instance or workflow segments are estimated effectively and efficiently with the support of four basic building blocks. Afterwards, through a negotiation process between service users and service providers based on either a time-oriented or a probability-oriented process, the coarse-grained temporal constraints are assigned first. With those coarse-grained temporal constraints, the fine-grained temporal constraints for individual workflow activities are derived in an automatic fashion. We demonstrated the effectiveness of our strategy through a case study.
- Chapter 7 presented the existing state-of-the-art checkpoint selection and temporal verification strategies which were modified to adapt to our probability-based temporal consistency model. Accordingly, new definitions, the minimum probability time redundancy based checkpoint selection strategy, and probability temporal consistency-based temporal verification strategy, are provided. Based on our improvement, only one type of checkpoint needs to be selected instead of previous multiple ones, and only one type of temporal consistency states needs to be verified instead of previous multiple ones. The theoretical proof has demonstrated that our adapted strategy is of the same necessity and sufficiency as the existing state-of-the-art checkpoint selection strategy but with better cost-effectiveness.
- Chapter 8 presented an adaptive temporal violation handling point selection strategy which is a novel idea presented in this book. Based on the selected necessary and sufficient checkpoints, we further select a subset of them where the probability of temporal violations is above a specific threshold, i.e. temporal violation handling is indeed necessary, as are temporal violation handling points. The simulation experiments demonstrated that our temporal violation handling point selection strategy can select much fewer temporal violation handling points than the conventional strategies while maintaining satisfactory temporal QoS.
- Chapter 9 presented an overview of temporal violation handling strategies for temporal violations. Given the basic requirements of *automation* and *cost-effectiveness*, we presented

a general two-stage local workflow rescheduling strategy which features a two-stage searching process with metaheuristic algorithms. Furthermore, two metaheuristics algorithms, viz. genetic algorithm (GA) and ant colony optimisation (ACO), are adapted and implemented in the general strategy, and then their performances are compared comprehensively. Furthermore, the three-level temporal violation handling strategy which consists of three levels of temporal violations, viz. level I, level II and level III, and their corresponding handling strategies, viz. *PTDA*, *ACOWR* and *PTDA + ACOWR*, is presented. The experimental results have shown that our strategy can ensure close to 0% global and local temporal violation rates, thus achieving high temporal QoS in scientific cloud workflow systems.

In summary, wrapping up all chapters, we can conclude that with the research results in this book, viz. a set of new concepts, innovative strategies and algorithms, our novel probabilistic temporal framework can significantly improve temporal QoS in scientific cloud workflow systems in a cost-effective fashion.

10.3   Contributions of This Book

The significance of this research is that we have designed a novel probabilistic framework which can provide a cost-effective lifecycle support for high temporal QoS in scientific cloud workflow systems. Specifically, it addresses some of the limitations in conventional temporal verification studies. The detailed analysis is conducted for each component of the temporal framework, viz. Component I − setting temporal constraints, Component II − monitoring temporal consistency and Component III − handling temporal violations. Based on the analysis, a set of new concepts such as a probability-based temporal consistency model, temporal violation handling point selection, innovative strategies and algorithms for the delivery of high temporal QoS have been presented and developed. Corresponding comparisons and quantitative evaluations have shown that these new concepts, innovative strategies and algorithms can significantly improve the level of temporal QoS in scientific cloud workflow systems. In the context of cloud economy, any resources consumed must be paid for. Improving temporal QoS would save more resources from temporal violation handling for executing scientific cloud workflows. Therefore, the research in this book would eventually improve overall performance and usability of scientific cloud workflow systems as our temporal framework can be viewed as a function or service of scientific cloud workflow systems. As a consequence, by deploying our new concepts, innovative strategies and algorithms, scientific cloud workflow systems would be able to better support large-scale sophisticated scientific applications in the context of cloud economy.

In particular, the major contributions of this book are:

1. Systematic analysis of the requirements for lifecycle support for high temporal QoS in scientific cloud workflow systems
   Unlike recent studies which focus only on checkpoint selection and temporal verification (i.e. part of Component II in our framework), this book has investigated the whole lifecycle support for high temporal QoS in scientific cloud workflow systems. At each step of the scientific cloud workflow lifecycle, this book has analysed the basic requirements

and the major problems in the conventional temporal verification work. For Component I (setting temporal constraints), this book has shown that the forecasting of accurate activity duration intervals is critical for all the components in the temporal framework, and user-defined global temporal constraints are not sufficient for fine-grained control. For Component II, this book has analysed the requirements for cost-effective monitoring of large-scale scientific cloud workflow instances. For Component III, this book has first analysed the necessity for temporal violation handling at every checkpoint. Afterwards, the requirements of *automation* and *cost-effectiveness* for temporal violation handling have been presented.

2. New probability-based temporal consistency model
   Based on the problem analysis for the conventional multi-state-based temporal consistency model, a new probability-based temporal consistency model has been presented where the range for statistically recoverable and non-recoverable temporal violations have been defined. The theoretical proof and experimental results have shown that our new presented temporal consistency model can achieve the same effectiveness as the conventional model in monitoring temporal consistency but with much better cost-effectiveness due to the decrease of checkpoint selection and temporal verification times.

3. A novel strategy for forecasting activity duration intervals based on statistical time-series patterns
   A novel forecasting strategy for scientific cloud workflow activity duration intervals has been developed. By analysing the specific requirements of data-/computation-intensive activities in scientific cloud workflow systems, statistical time-series-pattern-based forecasting strategies have been presented to overcome the limitation of conventional forecasting strategies and achieve better accuracy.

4. An innovative setting strategy for coarse-grained and fine-grained temporal constraints in scientific cloud workflow systems
   An innovative setting strategy has been presented in this book. The coarse-grained temporal constraints are assigned through either a time-oriented or a probability-oriented negotiation process between service users and service providers. Afterwards, based on those coarse-grained temporal constraints, fine-grained temporal constraints can be propagated along scientific cloud workflows in an automatic fashion.

5. A novel strategy for temporal violation handling point selection
   Conventional temporal verification work conducts temporal violation handling on every selected necessary and sufficient checkpoint. However, based on the analysis in this book, we have identified the phenomenon of self-recovery where minor temporal violations can usually be auto-recovered by the reduced execution time of the subsequent workflow activities. Therefore, a novel adaptive temporal violation handling point selection strategy has been presented to further select a subset of the checkpoints as temporal violation handling points for handling temporal violations. The experimental results have shown that our strategy can significantly reduce the times of temporal violation handling while maintaining satisfactory temporal correctness.

6. An innovative general metaheuristics-based workflow rescheduling strategy
   This book focuses on light-weight temporal violation handling strategies for recoverable temporal violations. Specifically, we have designed a general two-stage workflow local rescheduling strategy which utilises metaheuristics algorithms to optimise the integrated Task-Resource list. The general strategy has been further implemented with GA and ACO. The experimental results have shown that it can effectively compensate time deficits without recruiting additional resources.

Appendix: Notation Index

Symbols	Denotations
$\alpha\%C$	$\alpha\%$ Consistency (in the probability-based model)
a_i	The ith activity point of a scientific cloud workflow
AC	Absolute Consistency (in the probability-based model)
ACO	Ant Colony Optimisation
ACOWR	Ant Colony Optimisation-based two-stage local Workflow Rescheduling
AD	The adaptive temporal violation handling point selection strategy
AI	Absolute Inconsistency (in the probability-based model)
B_{ij}	The bias for mapping task a_i to resource R_j
$c\tau_{ij}$	The pheromone for the desirability of mapping task a_i to resource R_j from the perspective of execution cost
CompensationRatio	The compensation ratio of a rescheduling strategy
CPUTime	The CPU time of a rescheduling strategy
CSS	Checkpoint Selection Strategy
CSS_{TD}	The Temporal Dependency-based Checkpoint Selection Strategy
$d\tau_{ij}$	The pheromone for the desirability of mapping task a_i to resource R_j from the perspective of execution time
$D(a_i)$	The maximum duration of a_i
$d(a_i)$	The minimum duration of a_i
FitnessValue	The fitness value of a candidate solution with total
(TotalMakespan,TotalCost)	makespan (*TotalMakespan*) and total cost (*TotalCost*)
FT	The predefined fixed confidence threshold for self-recovery
GA	Genetic Algorithm
K	The initial value for equal segmentation
K-MaxSDev	A non-linear time-series segmentation algorithm
$L\{(a_i,R_j)\}$	An integrated Task-Resource list
$M(a_i)$	The mean duration of a_i
MaxSDev	The maximum standard deviation
Min_pattern_length	The minimum length threshold for a valid time-series pattern
$MPTR(a_p)$	The Minimum of all Probability Time Redundancies at a_p
$N(\mu_i,\sigma_i^2)$	A normal distribution model which has the expected value of μ_i and standard deviation of σ_i

(Continued)

Symbols	Denotations
NIL	The natural condition without temporal violation handling
OptMakespan	The optimisation ratio on total makespan
OptCost	The optimisation ratio on total cost
$Patterns = \{P_1, P_2, \ldots, P_m\}$	A set of time-series patterns which consists of m patterns
$PTD(U(SW), a_p)$	The Probability Time Deficit of $U(SW)$ at a_p
$PTR(U(SW), (a_{p+1}, a_{p+m}))$	The Probability Time Redundancy of workflow segment from a_{p+1} to a_{p+m} for $U(SW)$
$P(T)$	The probability of self-recovery
PT	The adaptive Probability Threshold for self-recovery
PTDA	Probability Time Deficit Allocation
$PTR(U(a_i, a_j), a_p)$	The Probability Time Redundancy of a_p for $U(a_i, a_j)$
QoS	Quality of Service
$R(a_i)$	The actual run-time duration of a_i
RA	The pure random handling point selection strategy
R_j	The jth resource
SC	Strong Consistency (in the multi-states-based model)
SI	Strong Inconsistency (in the multi-states-based model)
$T = \{X_1, X_2, \ldots, X_n\}$	A time series T which consists of n points
TDA	Time Deficit Allocation
$U(a_i)$	The upper bound temporal constraint for a_i
$U(SW)$	The upper bound temporal constraint for scientific workflow SW
WC	Weak Consistency (in the multi-states-based model)
WI	Weak Inconsistency (in the multi-states-based model)
μ	Sample mean
σ	Sample standard deviation
β	The probability for choosing the execution path
ρ	The probability for meeting the end conditions for a single iteration
$\theta\%$	The minimum acceptable temporal consistency
$\theta(a_p)$	The activity duration of a_p satisfying $\theta\%$ temporal consistency

Bibliography

[1] Academy of Technology Science and Engineering, Australia. Cloud computing: opportunities and challenges for Australia, <http://www.atse.org.au/component/remository/ATSE-Reports/Information-Technology/CLOUD-COMPUTING-Opportunities-and-Challenges-for-Australia-2010/> [accessed 1.09.01].

[2] W.M.P. van der Aalst, K.M.V. Hee, Workflow management: models, methods, and systems, The MIT Press, Cambridge, 2002.

[3] W.M.P. van der Aalst, K.M.V. Hee, H.A. Reijers, Analysis of discrete-time Stochastic Petri Nets, Statistica Neerlandica 54 (1) (2000) 237−255.

[4] S. Akioka, Y. Muraoka, Extended forecast of CPU and network load on computational grid. In: Proc. IEEE international symposium on cluster computing and the grid (CCGrid2004). Chicago, IL, USA; 2004. pp. 765−772.

[5] M. Armbrust, A. Fox, R. Griffith, A.D. Joseph, R.H. Katz, A. Konwinski, et al. Above the clouds: a Berkeley view of cloud computing. Technical report, University of California at Berkeley, <http://www.eecs.berkeley.edu/Pubs/TechRpts/2009/EECS-2009-28.pdf> [accessed 1.09.11].

[6] J. Behnamian, M. Zandieh, S.M.T. Fatemi Ghomi, Parallel-machine scheduling problems with sequence-dependent setup times using an ACO, SA and VNS hybrid algorithm, Expert Syst Appl 36 (6) (2009) 9637−9644.

[7] C. Blum, A. Roli, Metaheuristics in combinatorial optimization: overview and conceptual comparison, ACM Comput Surv 35 (3) (2003) 268−308.

[8] G. Boss, P. Malladi, D. Quan, L. Legregni, H. Hall, IBM cloud computing (White Paper). Technical report, <http://download.boulder.ibm.com/ibmdl/pub/software/dw/wes/hipods/Cloud_computing_wp_final_8Oct.pdf> [accessed 1.09.11].

[9] G. Bucci, L. Sassoli, E. Vicario, Correctness verification and performance analysis of real-time systems using stochastic preemptive time petri nets, IEEE Trans Softw Eng 31 (11) (2005) 913−927.

[10] P.A. Buhr, W.Y.R. Mok, Advanced exception handling mechanisms, IEEE Trans Softw Eng 26 (9) (2000) 820−836.

[11] R. Buyya, K. Bubendorfer, Market oriented grid and utility computing, Wiley Press, New York, NY, 2009.

[12] R. Buyya, C.S. Yeo, S. Venugopal, J. Broberg, I. Brandic, Cloud computing and emerging IT platforms: vision, hype, and reality for delivering computing as the 5th utility, Future Gener Comp Syst 25 (6) (2009) 599−616.

[13] R.-S. Chang, J.-S. Chang, P.-S. Lin, An ant algorithm for balanced job scheduling in grids, Future Gener Comp Syst 25 (1) (2009) 20−27.

[14] C. Chatfield, The analysis of time series: an introduction, 6th ed., Chapman and Hall/CRC, New York, NY, 2004.

[15] H. Che-Lun, Y. Don-Lin, C. Yeh-Ching, H. Ming-Chuan, A novel mining algorithm for periodic clustering sequential patterns. In: Proc. 19th international conference on industrial, engineering and other applications of applied intelligent systems (IEA/AIE2006). Annecy, France; 2006. pp. 1299−1308.

[16] J. Chen, Towards effective and efficient temporal verification in grid workflow systems, PhD thesis. Swinburne University of Technology, <http://www.researchbank.swinburne.edu.au/vital/access/manager/Repository/swin:7425> [accessed 1.09.11].

[17] J. Chen, Y. Yang, Localising temporal constraints in scientific workflows, J Comput Syst Sci 76 (6) (2010) 464−474.

[18] J. Chen, Y. Yang, Multiple states based temporal consistency for dynamic verification of fixed-time constraints in grid workflow systems, Concurrency Comput Pract Exper 19 (7) (2007) 965−982 [Wiley].

[19] J. Chen, Y. Yang, Activity completion duration based checkpoint selection for dynamic verification of temporal constraints in grid workflow systems, Int J High Perform Comput Appl 22 (3) (2008) 319−329.

[20] J. Chen, Y. Yang, A taxonomy of grid workflow verification and validation, Concurrency Comput Pract Exper 20 (4) (2008) 347−360.

[21] J. Chen, Y. Yang, Temporal dependency based checkpoint selection for dynamic verification of temporal constraints in scientific workflow systems, ACM Trans Softw Eng Meth 20 (3) (2011) [article 9].

[22] J. Chen, Y. Yang, Adaptive selection of necessary and sufficient checkpoints for dynamic verification of temporal constraints in grid workflow systems, ACM Trans Autonomous Adaptive Syst 2 (2) (2007) [article 6].

[23] J. Chen, Y. Yang, Temporal dependency based checkpoint selection for dynamic verification of fixed-time constraints in grid workflow systems, In: Proc. 30th international conference on software engineering (ICSE2008). Leipzig, Germany; 2008. pp. 141−150.

[24] J. Chen, Y. Yang, T.Y. Chen, Dynamic verification of temporal constraints on-the-fly for workflow systems, In: Proc. 11th Asia-Pacific software engineering conference. Busan, Korea; 2004. pp. 30−37.

[25] T.Y. Chen, R. Merkel, An upper bound on software testing effectiveness, ACM Trans Softw Eng Meth 17 (3) (2008) 1−27.

[26] W-N. Chen, J. Zhang, Y. Yu, Workflow scheduling in grids: an ant colony optimization approach. In: Proc. 2007 IEEE congress on evolutionary computation (CEC2007). Singapore; 2007. pp. 3308−3315.

[27] W-N. Chen, J. Zhang, An ant colony optimization approach to a grid scheduling problem with various QoS requirements, IEEE Trans Systems, Man and Cybernetics, Part C: Applications and Reviews, 39 (1) (2009) 29−43.

[28] P. Choudhury, R. Kumar, P.P. Chakrabarti, Hybrid scheduling of dynamic task graphs with selective duplication for multiprocessors under memory and time constraints, IEEE Trans Parallel Distr Syst 19 (7) (2008) 967−980.

[29] E. Commission. The future of cloud computing, opportunities for European cloud computing beyond 2010, <http://cordis.europa.eu/fp7/ict/%20ssai/docs/cloud-report-final.pdf> [accessed 1.09.11].

[30] K. Cooper, A. Dasgupta, K. Kennedy, C. Koelbel, A. Mandal, New grid scheduling and rescheduling methods in the GrADS project. In: Proc. 18th international parallel and distributed processing symposium (IPDPS2004). Santa Fe, NM, USA; 2004. pp. 199−206.

[31] DAGMan, Condor Project, <http://www.cs.wisc.edu/condor/> [accessed 1.09.11].

[32] E. Deelman, D. Gannon, M. Shields, I. Taylor, Workflows and e-science: an overview of workflow system features and capabilities, Future Gener Comp Syst 25 (6) (2008) 528−540.

[33] Department of Finance and Deregulation, Australian Government: Cloud Computing Strategic Direction Paper, <http://www.finance.gov.au/e-government/strategy-andgovernance/cloud-computing.html> [accessed 1.09.11].

[34] P.A. Dinda, D.R. O'Hallaron, Host load prediction using linear models, Cluster Comput 3 (4) (2000) 265−280.

[35] M. Dobber, R. van der Mei, G. Koole, A prediction method for job runtimes on shared processors: survey, statistical analysis and new avenues, Performance Evaluation 64 (7−8) (2007) 755−781.

[36] M. Dobber, R. van der Mei, G. Koole, Statistical properties of task running times in a global-scale grid environment. In: Proc. 6th IEEE international symposium on cluster computing and the grid (CCGRID06). Singapore; 2006. vol. 1, pp. 150−153.

[37] J. Eder, E. Panagos, M. Rabinovich, Time constraints in workflow systems. In: Proc. 11th international conference on advanced information systems engineering (CAiSE99). Heidelberg, Germany; 1999. pp. 286−300.

[38] T. Erl, SOA: principles of service design, Prentice Hall, Boston, MA, 2008.

[39] B. Fechner, U. Honig, J. Keller, W. Schiffmann, Fault-tolerant static scheduling for grids. In: Proc. 2008 IEEE international parallel and distributed processing symposium (IPDPS2008). Miami, FL, USA; 2008. pp. 1−6.

[40] S. Ferretti, V. Ghini, F. Panzieri, M. Pellegrini, E. Turrini, QoS-aware clouds. In: Proc. IEEE 3rd international conference on cloud computing; 2010. pp. 321−328.

[41] I. Foster, Z. Yong, I. Raicu, S. Lu, Cloud computing and grid computing 360-degree compared. In: Proc. 2008 grid computing environments workshop (GCE08). Austin, TX, USA; 2008. pp. 1−10.

[42] The Apache Software Foundation, MapReduce, <http://hadoop.apache.org/> ; mapreduce/ [accessed 1.11.10].

[43] C. Fu-Lai, F. Tak-Chung, V. Ng, R.W.P. Luk, An evolutionary approach to pattern-based time series segmentation, IEEE Trans Evolut Comput 8 (5) (2004) 471−489.

[44] C. Glasner, J. Volkert, Adaps − a three-phase adaptive prediction system for the run-time of jobs based on user behaviour, J Comput Syst Sci (2010)10.1016/j.jcss.2010.01.005 [in press].

[45] Hadoop, <http://hadoop.apache.org/> [accessed 1.09.11].

[46] C. Hagen, G. Alonso, Exception handling in workflow management systems, IEEE Trans Softw Eng 26 (10) (2000) 943−958.

[47] J.W. Han, M. Kamber, Data mining: concepts and techniques, 2nd ed., Elsevier, San Francisco, CA 94111, 2006.

[48] HPGC, Proc. 6th high-performance grid computing workshop in conjunction with 23rd parallel and distributed processing symposium (IPDPS09). Rome, Italy; 2009.

[49] Y.-P. Huang, C.-C. Hsu, S.-H. Wang, Pattern recognition in time series database: a case study on financial database, Expert Syst Appl 33 (1) (2007) 199−205.

[50] S.Y. Hwang, H. Wang, J. Tang, J. Srivastava, A probabilistic approach to modelling and estimating the QoS of web-services-based workflows, Inform Sci 177 (23) (2007) 5484−5503.

[51] IBM, Understanding quality of service for web services, <http://www.ibm.com/developer works/library/ws-quality.html> [accessed 1.09.11].

[52] B. Kao, H. Garcia-Molina, Deadline assignment in a distributed soft real-time system, IEEE Trans Parallel Distr Syst 8 (12) (1997) 1268−1274.

[53] E. Keogh, S. Chu, D. Hart, M. Pazzani, An online algorithm for segmenting time series. In: Proc. 2001 IEEE international conference on data mining (ICDM2001), San Jose, CA, USA; 2001. pp. 289−296.

[54] A.M. Law, W.D. Kelton, Simulation modelling and analysis, 4th ed., McGraw-Hill, New York, NY, 2007.

[55] Z. Liangzhao, B. Benatallah, A.H.H. Ngu, M. Dumas, J. Kalagnanam, H. Chang, QoS-aware middleware for web services composition, IEEE Trans Softw Eng. 30 (5) (2004) 311−327.

[56] SAP Library, Workflow System Administration, <http://help.sap.com/>; saphelp_nw2004s/helpdata/en [accessed 1.09.11].

[57] L. Yang, I. Foster, J.M. Schopf, Homeostatic and tendency-based CPU load predictions, In: Proc. 2003 international parallel and distributed processing symposium (IPDPS2003). Nice, France; 2003.

[58] K. Liu, H. Jin, J. Chen, X. Liu, D. Yuan, Y. Yang, A compromised-time-cost scheduling algorithm in SwinDeW-C for instance-intensive cost-constrained workflows on cloud computing platform, Inter J High Perform Comput Appl 24 (4) (2010) 445−456.

[59] X. Liu, J. Chen, K. Liu, Y. Yang, Forecasting duration intervals of scientific workflow activities based on time-series patterns, In: Proc. 4th IEEE international conference on e-science (e-Science08). Indianapolis, IN, USA; 2008. pp. 23−30.

[60] X. Liu, J. Chen, Z. Wu, Z. Ni, D. Yuan, Y. Yang, Handling recoverable temporal violations in scientific workflow systems: a workflow rescheduling based strategy, In: Proc. 10th IEEE/ACM international symposium on cluster, cloud and grid computing (CCGRID10). Melbourne, Australia; 2010. pp. 534−537.

[61] X. Liu, J. Chen, Y. Yang, A probabilistic strategy for setting temporal constraints in scientific workflows. In: 6th international Conference on business process management (BPM08). Milan, Italy; 2008. pp. 180−195.

[62] X. Liu, Z. Ni, J. Chen, Y. Yang, A probabilistic strategy for temporal constraint management in scientific workflow systems. Concurrency and computation: practice and experience [online], <http://onlinelibrary.wiley.com/doi/10.1002/cpe.1739/pdf> [accessed 1.09.11].

[63] X. Liu, Z. Ni, Z. Wu, D. Yuan, J. Chen, Y. Yang, An effective framework of lightweight handling for three-level fine-grained recoverable temporal violations in scientific workflows. In: Proc. 16th IEEE international conference on parallel and distributed systems (ICPADS2010). Shanghai, China; 2010. pp. 43−50.

[64] X. Liu, Z. Ni, Z. Wu, D. Yuan, J. Chen, Y. Yang, A novel general framework for automatic and cost-effective handling of recoverable temporal violations in scientific workflow systems, J Syst Softw 84 (3) (2011) 492−509 [Elsevier].

[65] X. Liu, Z. Ni, D. Yuan, Y. Jiang, Z. Wu, J. Chen, et al., A novel statistical time-series pattern based interval forecasting strategy for activity durations in workflow systems, J Syst Softw. 84 (3) (2011) 354−376 [Elsevier].

[66] X. Liu, Y. Yang, J. Chen, Q. Wang, M. Li, Achieving on-time delivery: a two-stage probabilistic scheduling strategy for software projects. In: Proc. 2009 international conference on software process: trustworthy software development processes. Vancouver, Canada; 2009.

[67] X. Liu, Y. Yang, Y. Jiang, J. Chen, Preventing temporal violations in scientific workflows: where and how, IEEE Trans Softw Eng (2010) [online].

[68] X. Liu, D. Yuan, G. Zhang, J. Chen, Y. Yang, SwinDeW-C: a peer-to-peer based cloud workflow system, in: B. Furht, A. Escalante (Eds.), Handbook of cloud computing, Springer, New York, USA, 2010, pp. 309−332.

[69] O. Marjanovic, M.E. Orlowska, On modelling and verification of temporal constraints in production workflows, Know Inform Syst 1 (2) (1999) 157−192.

[70] A. Martinez, F.J. Alfaro, J.L. Sanchez, F.J. Quiles, J. Duato, A new cost-effective technique for QoS support in clusters, IEEE Trans Parallel Distr Syst 18 (12) (2007) 1714−1726.

[71] M. Moore, An accurate parallel genetic algorithm to schedule tasks on a cluster, Parallel Comput 30 (2004) 567−583.

[72] S. Nadarajah, S. Kotz, Exact distribution of the max/min of two Gaussian random variables, IEEE Trans Very Large Scale Integration Syst 16 (2) (2008) 210−212.

[73] F. Nadeem, T. Fahringer, Using templates to predict execution time of scientific workflow applications in the grid. In: Proc. 2009 IEEE/ACM international symposium on cluster computing and the grid (CCGRID09). Shanghai, China; 2009. pp. 316−323.

[74] F. Nadeem, M.M. Yousaf, R. Prodan, T. Fahringer, Soft benchmarks-based application performance prediction using a minimum training set. In: Proc. 2nd IEEE international conference on e-science and grid computing (e-Science06). Amsterdam, Netherlands; 2006.

[75] J. Oh, C. Wu, Genetic-algorithm-based real-time task scheduling with multiple goals, J Syst Softw 71 (2004) 245−258.

[76] PDSEC. Proc. 10th IEEE international workshop on parallel and distributed scientific and engineering computing, in conjunction with 23rd parallel and distributed processing symposium (IPDPS09). Rome, Italy; 2009.

[77] R. Prodan, T. Fahringer, Overhead analysis of scientific workflows in grid environments, IEEE Trans Parallel Distr Syst 19 (3) (2008) 378−393.

[78] Askalon Project, <http://www.dps.uibk.ac.at/projects/askalon> [accessed 1.09.11].

[79] CROWN Project, CROWN portal, <http://www.crown.org.cn/en/> [accessed 1.09.11].

[80] GridBus Project, <http://www.gridbus.org> [accessed 1.09.11].

[81] JOpera Project, <http://www.iks.ethz.ch/jopera> [accessed 1.09.11].

[82] Kepler Project, <http://kepler-project.org/> [accessed 1.09.11].

[83] Triana Project, <http://www.trianacode.org/> [accessed 1.09.11].

[84] Taverna Project, <http://www.mygrid.org.uk/tools/taverna/> [accessed 1.09.11].

[85] UNICORE Project, <http://www.unicore.eu/> [accessed 1.09.11].

[86] K. Ren, X. Liu, J. Chen, N. Xiao, J. Song, W. Zhang, A QSQL-based efficient planning algorithm for fully-automated service composition in dynamic service environments. In: Proc. 2008 IEEE international conference on services computing (SCC08). Honolulu, HI, USA; 2008. pp. 301−308.

[87] N. Russell, W.M.P. van der Aalst, A.H.M. ter Hofstede, Exception handling patterns in process-aware information systems. Technical report BPM-06-04, <http://www.work-flowpatterns.com/documentation/documents/BPM-06-04.pdf> ; 2006.

[88] N. Russell, W.M.P. van der Aalst, A.H.M. ter Hofstede, Workflow exception patterns. In: Proc. 18th international conference on advanced information systems engineering (CAiSE06). Luxembourg; 2006. pp. 288−302.

[89] SECES, Proc. 1st international workshop on software engineering for computational science and engineering, in conjunction with 30th international conference on software engineering (ICSE2008). Leipzig, Germany; 2008.

[90] W. Smith, I. Foster, V. Taylor, Predicting application run times with historical information, J Parallel Distr Comput 64 (9) (2004) 1007−1016.

[91] J.H. Son, J. Sun Kim, M.Ho Kim, Extracting the workflow critical path from the extended well-formed workflow schema, J Comput Syst Sci 70 (1) (2005) 86−106.

[92] K.A. Stroud, Engineering mathematics, 6th ed., Palgrave Macmillan, Basingstoke, 2007.

[93] I.J. Taylor, E. Deelman, D.B. Gannon, M. Shields, Workflows for e-science: scientific workflows for grids, Springer, London, 2007.

[94] S. Tirthapura, B. Xu, C. Busch, Sketching asynchronous streams over a sliding window. In: Proc. 25th annual ACM symposium on principles of distributed computing (PODC06). Denver, CO, USA; 2006. pp. 82−91.

[95] D.B. Tracy, J.S. Howard, B. Noah, Comparison of eleven static heuristics for mapping a class of independent tasks onto heterogeneous distributed computing systems, J Parallel Distr Comput 61 (6) (2001) 810−837.

[96] VMware, <http://www.vmware.com/> [accessed 1.09.11].

[97] L. Wang, W. Jie, J. Chen, Grid computing: infrastructure, service, and applications, CRC Press, Taylor & Francis Group, Boca Raton, FL 33487, 2009.

[98] R. Wolski, Forecasting network performance to support dynamic scheduling using the network weather service. In: Proc. 6th IEEE international symposium on high performance distributed computing (HPDC97). Portland, OR, USA; 1997. pp. 316−325.

[99] Z. Wu, X. Liu, Z. Ni, D. Yuan, Y. Yang, A market-oriented hierarchical scheduling strategy in cloud workflow systems, J Supercomput (2011) [online] [accessed 1.09.11].

[100] Y. Yang, K. Liu, J. Chen, J. Lignier, H. Jin, Peer-to-peer based grid workflow runtime environment of SwinDeW-G. In: Proc. 3rd international conference on e-science and grid computing (e-Science07). Bangalore, India; 2007. pp. 51−58.

[101] Y. Yang, K. Liu, J. Chen, X. Liu, D. Yuan, H. Jin, An algorithm in SwinDeW-C for scheduling transaction-intensive cost-constrained cloud workflows. In: Proc. 4th IEEE international conference on e-science (e-Science08). Indianapolis, IN, USA; 2008. pp. 374−375.

[102] W. Yongwei, Y. Yulai, Y. Guangwen, Z. Weimin, Load prediction using hybrid model for computational grid. In: Proc. 8th IEEE/ACM international conference on grid computing (Grid07). Austin, TX, USA; 2007. pp. 235−242.

[103] J. Yu, R. Buyya, A taxonomy of workflow management systems for grid computing, J Grid Comput (3) (2005) 171−200.

[104] J. Yu, R. Buyya, Scheduling scientific workflow applications with deadline and budget constraints using genetic algorithms, Scientific Program 14 (3) (2006) 217−230.

[105] J. Yu, R. Buyya, Workflow scheduling algorithms for grid computing, in: F. Xhafa, A. Abraham (Eds.), Metaheuristics for scheduling in distributed computing environments, Springer, Berlin, 2008.

[106] Z. Yu, W. Shi, An adaptive rescheduling strategy for grid workflow applications. In: Proc. 2007 IEEE international symposium on parallel and distributed processing (IPDPS2007). Long Beach, CA, USA; 2007; pp. 115−122.

[107] L. Zhang, Y. Chen, B. Yang, Task scheduling based on PSO algorithm in computational grid. In: Proc. 6th international conference on intelligent systems design and applications (ISDA2006). Jinan, China; 2006. vol. 2, pp. 696−701.

[108] Y. Zhang, W. Sun, Y. Inoguchi, Predict task running time in grid environments based on cpu load predictions, Future Gener Comput Syst 24 (6) (2008) 489−497.

[109] Y.Y. Zhang, W. Sun, Y. Inoguchi, Predicting running time of grid tasks based on CPU load predictions. In: Proc. 2006 IEEE international conference on grid computing. Barcelona, Spain; 2006. pp. 286−292.

[110] H. Zhuge, T. Cheung, H. Pung, A timed workflow process model, J Syst Softw 55 (3) (2001) 231−243.

Printed and bound by CPI Group (UK) Ltd, Croydon, CR0 4YY

03/10/2024

01040413-0011